Bloom

WHERE YOU'RE PLANTED

Exploring stories of encouragement and strength in the
lives of women in church planting.

ANNE MILAM

ISBN-13: 978-1484043073
ISBN-10: 1484043073

TABLE OF CONTENTS

PRUNING

STORMS

WEEDING

SEEDLINGS

BLOSSOMING

GARDNER'S NOTES

ACKNOWLEDGEMENTS
by Anne Milam

No one writes a book alone and that is especially true in this instance. I would like to recognize and thank the women of Bloom who contributed to the chapters found in this book. By sharing their stories with me, I in turn, was able to share them with you. Their authenticity and transparency about how church planting has shaped their lives is what makes this book an invaluable tool.

I would also like to thank my friend, Debbie Jones, the director of Bloom Ministries. She planted the seed for this book in my heart and watered it consistently over the past year. Her persevering encouragement and prayer when I was feeling fear and overwhelming doubt enabled me to complete this task. Thank you for believing in me.

To my church family at Kinetic Church, I truly love doing life with you. I am so thankful that God called David and me out of our comfort zone to plant a church of disciples who make disciples. Never loose the mission.

Finally, I want to recognize my amazing family. I want thank my kids for dealing with a mom who on many days was pajama clad and totally glued to her computer most of the day. Thank you for dealing with a mom on "Book Brain" all year long. And to David, my husband, best friend, and fabulous book cover designer, thank you for your belief that I could do this. Thank you for your unwavering support and your great eye for design. You listened when I told you what I was wanted in a cover and made it better than I could imagine. I love doing life with you, even the hard stuff.

INTRODUCTION

by Anne Milam

"The Glory of God is man fully alive!" - St. Irenaeus

When God calls us on a difficult journey, He doesn't just do it because He has a cosmic want ad that He needs filled. He calls us to out of the way places, or to busy, crowded spaces, to journey's that are dangerous and filled with heartache because He wants so much more for us than we can comprehend. He wants us fully alive and dangerous to the enemy.

God knows that if we stay comfortable, content, and cozy, like hobbits in the Shire, we will never know His fierce, abiding, dangerous love. We will never have faith that can move mountains, we will never cling to Him alone and we will never dive into battles with odds so clearly stacked against us.

It is in those moments, when things are dire and we are faithful, that we actually become the best vessels for his glory. God is most magnified when we are hard pressed, shaken down, and oppressed. Only when we are finally mashed up so small that there is barely any room left for us, is there room for God's glory to encompass and wash over us, spilling out on all who pass by.

This book is about God's glory revealed in women who answer that call in a uniquely fearsome way. It is about pastor's wives, more specifically, it is the story of leaders who step out in faith, and leaving everything solid and secure behind them, partner with their husbands in planting new churches.

Blooming where you are planted is one of the most difficult things any woman can do. Being uprooted from all you hold dear can take it's toll. But if you are blooming, you are thriving. You are beautiful to behold wherever you have been planted.

If you have been called on this difficult journey, remember above all else, *you are not alone!* And I don't just mean that Jesus is with you always. I mean there are women today doing what you are doing and thriving. Never forget that a great cloud of witnesses has gone before you over the ages. Women who have bloomed on the mission field, in the New World, on the prairie, out West, across the seas, in Rome. We are the lucky ones, we live in a time when communication and encouragement between other women walking this same journey is easy.

This book is about the journey of a church planting wife, a pastor's wife. A woman who chooses to bring beauty and peace to those around her, by blooming recklessly where God has planted her.

TRANSPLANTING

trans·plant·ing [trans-plant-ing, -plahnt] *v.* **1.** to remove (a plant) from one place and plant it in another. **2.** to move from one place to another. **3.** to bring a family from one country, region, etc., to another for settlement; relocate.

HOW DID I GET HERE?

by Anne Milam

Have you ever driven down the road on auto pilot and looked up only to think in a moment of panic, "Where am I?" "How did I get here?" This happens to me a lot, well maybe not a lot, but often enough to be mentioned. Maybe it's because I start day dreaming while driving the same stretch of highway repeatedly. It's kind of fun to imagine I'm a rock star belting out the song on my iPhone via car stereo, while driving down the road in a 12 year old Honda mini van, carrying 4 bickering children, on the way to set up and tear down church each Sunday.

But I digress.

How did I get to this juncture? How did I become a church planting wife? Well, it all started with church camp, where many great things have been known to begin.

I have been a devout church camper ever since I was in third grade when I attended a half week of camp for newbies. I loved how amazing the worship was at and how close to God I felt. I thought the lifeguard was super cute and I felt an illicit thrill at being allowed to drink soda and eat a candy bar every single afternoon. I loved the silly games and disgusting challenges, like licking peanut butter out of the dean's armpit to earn your 3 letters from Mom. (This was back in the days before seatbelt laws and bike helmets.)

It was while at church camp that I became convicted of what I already knew, and decided to give my life to Christ. It was where I decided to go to Christian college. It was where I met and fell in love with Dave Milam, who became my husband. So it isn't too far of a stretch to find that after college, I was married to a youth minister who eventually became the dean of high school church camp.

My eldest son spent a week at church camp, with the huge help of our MeeMee, before he was a year old. When my daughter came along, she went to camp too. I found out I was preggers with my third child...at church camp. That year, 2003, was our 10 year anniversary. Since our June wedding date usually fell during or around the week of camp, we took an anniversary cruise to celebrate in May. Voila, a month and a half later at camp, the little stick turned pink!

But we weren't just pregnant with our third child. It was during that week that the seed of church planting was sown into my husband's heart. And that is where the church planting bit comes in. See, one of the best things about camp is hanging with all your other ministry friends that you never have time to meet with because you are all too busy in your own churches. Even if you live in the same city or region, it's hard to make time to connect. During the week of camp there is this exchange of ministry joys and sorrows, ideas and plans. One of these friends was considering church planting. He talked to David about it and encouraged him to check it out too.

So kind of on a whim, just to see what all the fuss was about, Dave called the number of the church planting guy. We hadn't really discussed it, as a couple, you know. Dave had sort of mentioned it in passing, just generally. He was curious, and made a call. The next thing you know, I was handed a stack of church planter assessment paperwork to fill out!

Alright, perhaps it wasn't quite that sudden, except that it was. One minute I am planning my third pregnancy, fully entrenched in the overwhelming but comfortable world of mothering a 2 and 4 year old, and the next I am being informed that we have the "opportunity" to go to assessment, where they decide if we are fit for leading a church plant or not. Sort of a shortened Christian version of Parris Island. "Are you one of the few, the proud, the chosen: Church Planters?"

That is like dangling bait on a hook for guys wired up for leadership. But first, I had to fill out this herculean pile of papers and surveys so they could make sure we were not crazy and that we wouldn't run off with any money they might entrust to us. Apparently, that had happened in these situations before.

I was not sure I was completely on board with all of this. I was exhausted from my first trimester and from chasing around a toddler and preschooler. I didn't really want to be a church planter, so why even go through all the hoops just to say "no" in the end anyway?

Some of you church planting wives and spiritual gurus out there, those of you who were excited to lead a plant from the get-go, are reading this thinking, "She was too comfortable in her nice suburban church." Let me explain where I was coming from. I was *extremely* comfortable and content at our former church. I felt *very* safe and secure. My children had been born while serving there. I had wonderful pediatricians, a fabulous OBGYN, and a dream of a dentist. My eldest child was all set to attend kindergarten at a great school. I had a huge network of free, safe, childcare providers: my sister, an adopted auntie, an adopted grandmother, her teenage daughter, and extended family within 2-4 hours. My father was struggling with mini strokes and being the eldest child, it fell to me to help organize his medical information and bills. Oh, and did I mention I was pregnant with our third child? You may think I lacked faith that God would work things out. That I was way too mainstream, entrenched even. Well, you would probably be right. But that was all about to change.

Knowing my mindset, I can now candidly share with you how maliciously I filled out each form and questionnaire I found in that stack of paperwork. I realize you may judge me by these dark corners of my heart, but I will share them anyway.

It occurred to me that if they, the assessment team, knew every dark, terrible secret I held, they may find me unfit to plant a church. So I set about answering each question as thoroughly and truthfully unvarnished as I possibly could. I didn't hide this intent from my husband Dave either, but he didn't seem worried.

Marveling at the weird questions on the psychiatric test, I plowed through statements like, "I have been on the cover of a magazine this year," or "I fly transatlantically on a weekly basis." Both were True/False questions. Or how about, "I am a very important person." How do you answer that? In light of God's truth, I would say, "True," but at the risk of sounding vain and narcissistic. Or worse, do I say, "False," and appear to have no self confidence? Then there were pages and pages of background and family history questions. When I complained, David reminded me that he had to fill out about twice as many forms as I did. Finally, we completed every form and sent them off hopefully. He, hoping they would accept, and me, hoping they would see how totally wrecked we were and unable to do this task.

Much to my dismay, we got a call a couple of weeks later. When would we be available to attend the assessment? Seriously? Were these people crazy? Maybe they hadn't read through all the material yet. Three months pregnant, I grudgingly agreed to go. I had no idea what God was going to do in my heart during that week of assessment.

That was the week I was reminded of why I had chosen to go to a Christian college in the first place. I was reminded of the call of my Savior on my heart to serve Him and Him alone. That week I was broken and then renewed and reset on the mission to make disciples who make disciples. It was kind of a Matrix moment, you know? You can take the blue pill and continue on in ignorant bliss or you can take the red pill and face the harsh reality, but really be alive. I chose the red pill.

Gratefully, things did not change all at once. We attended assessment in the fall of 2003 and they wanted us to move to Charlotte, NC, in February of 2004. Well, I was due with that third baby in February, remember? I felt totally incapable of being ready to make the transition on that timeline. God was gracious with me and the timeline was moved back. I was able to deliver the baby with my wonderful doctor. We were able to inform our church and elders and seek their support. We sold our home in three weeks and began to look for homes in Charlotte. Things were progressing. Then we were tempted. Or maybe I was tempted.

When Dave gave the elders in Indiana his resignation, we thought that was it. Unbeknownst to us, during the same elders meeting that they received our resignation, they also "let go" of our senior pastor at the time. I don't know all of the reasons or causes for that situation, but I do know that a few days later an elder was at our door offering us the lead pastorate, asking us to please reconsider.

I am a little ashamed to admit this, I know I said I chose the red pill, but seriously, can't we reach lost people here and meet Dave's God given desire to lead? Maybe God was giving us this opportunity to stay, now that He had tested us and found us faithful? It was possible, wasn't it? Honey, could you please, please make very, very sure that this is what God is calling us to? At least take time to consider this offer before just brushing it and everything stable aside.

Again God was so patient and kind with me. And so was David. He agreed to take a couple of weeks to think and pray about this decision. I promised him that if he would carefully consider his options, pray and seek counsel from friends in ministry, I would pray too and agree with whatever he felt compelled to do. After all, at that time all I really wanted to do was be a wife and mommy. I knew I could do that wherever God called us. And this time, I meant it.

Before long we were looking at houses in Charlotte. We had a short list of things we really wanted in a home; the kids wanted steps (an upstairs and downstairs), Dave wanted a fireplace, but high on my list was a place to plant blackberry bushes and a yard for the kids. One of our elders and his wife, back in Indiana, were good friends and they had blackberry bushes in their backyard. She made the most wonderful blackberry cobbler every 4th of July and I wanted to continue the tradition if at all possible.

The week we were in Charlotte was exhausting. We looked and looked and searched and searched for just the right house with our four month old needing to nurse every few hours in the back seat of the realtor's car. Finally, on the last day, we looked at a simple two story house in a pretty neighborhood. It had a fireplace, enough bedrooms and baths, good school district. But what sealed the deal came as I walked through the back door and around the side of the house. There, already planted, mature and bearing violet berries, was a blackberry patch. And I heard God speaking quietly into my heart, "See Anne, more than you could have ever hoped or asked for!"

- TRANSPLANTING -
SMALL THINGS
by Tammy Smith

I remember the day like it was yesterday. It was a Friday evening in January 1999. Two weeks prior, I had graduated and earned my Physical Therapy degree. Barry was returning from a week long class at Cincinnati Christian University. He walks in the front door and says, 'Honey we need to talk'. This was before kids, when we had plenty of time to talk. So when he said this, I knew it meant a full concentration, no distraction talk that would take place right away.

We sat on the sofa and he started talking about this class on leadership, and listening to a 'cheesy tape' that was Bill Hybels sharing from his heart. He explained how God spoke to him and that it was clear as day, how he had to fight back tears many times in this classroom, sitting with 15 other people who were falling asleep. Then Barry said it, "Honey, I think we need to plant a church. I think God wants us to plant a church!" I was stunned and it showed on my face. Barry stopped and started explaining again why he thought this.

Then he said, "We can plant in California, where 97% of the people there are non-churched and need Jesus." If I was not stunned before, when he said *California*, I was not breathing. You want me to move over 2500 miles away, to a state I have never visited and with people I think are all a bunch of 'fruits and nuts' to start a church in our living room? Really?

Needless to say we had multiple conversations about this matter and lots of prayer together and separately. In May, we took a vacation and flew to California and went through three days of assessments - talk about emotionally draining! In June, we took our 225 plus youth group to youth summer conference called Christ in Youth. By the first part of July we had accepted the call to plant a church with Stadia together, unified and as one! We resigned with our senior pastor's blessing in early July.

The following Wednesday morning, I woke up and took a test to realize we were pregnant with our first child. A total surprise! Not part of our plan for sure. We were not trying, but God had other plans. If we had only known this 4 days earlier. Or not. I'm not sure we would have resigned from a healthy church that had a thriving and growing youth ministry. God and his sense of humor. We didn't find it funny at the time. We questioned our calling and the timing. We sought wisdom from others. It was difficult having some of our family not happy that we were moving the only grand baby 2500 plus miles away. It was a confusing time during which we relied on our 'calling'.

September came, and with it was the time of very sad goodbyes and sobbing. It was not fun to leave all that was comfortable and safe. I remember driving away in a U-haul that had everything we owned on this earth in it. Our first stop was to sign the sale papers on our house. Then on to my parents' house in Kansas City, Missouri.

We finally made it to California. I was pregnant and was sick the entire 9 months. We lived in an apartment. It was during that time I really questioned what we had done. I may have even fallen into a slight depression, sleeping a lot, all in the name of being pregnant. Through it all, God was faithful and my husband was there. He worked so hard knowing that God had called us and God's calling doesn't go void. We finally moved into a house and found a place to hold Sunday worship services. Impact Community Church's grand opening was to be on March 12, 2000. We were so jazzed. Our son was due on February 23, giving us a few weeks to enjoy one birth before our second birth; the birth of Impact.

Again, things didn't go as we had planned. Our son decided to wait and make his grand appearance on Saturday morning, March 11. This was approximately 18 hours before Impact would have its first church service! This was wonderful and emotional all at once. Max, our son, and I didn't make it to the grand opening of Impact. Barry was going on very little sleep. I had been in labor for 26 hours including a night shift.

Again, God showed up and used Barry's emotions on the grand opening of Impact to relate to many women and we later learned it made Barry more approachable.

It was all God's timing and He was in control.

Church planting has been like a roller coaster ride! You have ups and downs and sometimes, OK a lot of times, you have no idea what direction you will go or how you will react to it. However, through it all, God's calling in our life has been loud and clear. He called Barry and I to plant and be obedient even when there were many times people thought we were crazy and even tried to talk us out of it. Looking back on our planting experience, there are many times, more then I care to admit to, that I wonder, how did we do that? How did we survive and not give up? And many times I think of this simple truth:

Many people *want* to do great things for God. But doing great things for God is being *faithful* in the very small things He asks us to do. Just like young Billy Graham and the bus driver who drove him to church every Sunday. Who did greater things for God? Billy Graham, or the bus driver who made it possible for Billy to hear the message of salvation? You decide.

In the mean time, Barry and I hold fast to the promise of God's calling in our lives and the promise we read in Jude 24 and 25 (MSG);

And now to him who can keep you on your feet, standing tall in his bright presence, fresh and celebrating-to our one God, our only Savior, through Jesus Christ, our Master, and rule before all time, and now, and to the end of all time. Yes!

Enough said. Enjoy the journey and rest in Him who has called you!

A SENSE OF PLACE

by Vanessa Bush

We rounded a bend in I-40 and emerged from a canyon to overlook the city we would call our new home. After three days of driving and way too much fast food, my legs ached, but the cries of my tired body could not be heard over the whispers of my satisfied soul. I was home. Strangely enough, this eccentric city, Albuquerque, with its scorched air and its spicy smells and all the beautiful bronze skin, felt familiar. God has a way of calming the spirit when we are in the center of his will.

Six months. Six months until a tiny church would take its first breath. We had six months to plan and prepare . . . and six months to just be in our new space. We had been sent by a church we loved, but it was a big church where busyness pervades and so many souls required attention. Our lives had grown loud and cloudy. We set out prepared to check off the long church launch "to do list" of boxes developed by some dear, organized person. But the most important thing I did to prepare to open those church doors was to scrub the hurry out of my heart. We lived as tourists in our new land and took a Sabbath from church work. The landscape and the denizens became my teachers, and I their eager student.

I shook hands with this new city, and she introduced herself. The high desert mesa said, "Come explore. You think you know a desert, but have you seen my unexpected beauty, my little bits of hope in the barrenness?" The famed Rio Grande beckoned, "Discover me, a haven and a refuge throughout the ages. Watch my Bosque leaves change from vibrant fall yellow then dull winter brown to emergent spring green and then the full emerald of summer as I meander the same path, always faithful." And the majestic Sandia mountains called out, "Come climb my rocks. Enjoy the cool breeze on my peaks fluttering the Aspens and caressing the wildflowers, a sweet relief from the pounding heat below. Watch as I reflect the pink sunset, my everyday reminder to be slow and savor." God told me a story of himself through my new surroundings.

One day we hiked the petroglyphs. I could reach out and touch ancient rock carvings dating back to the time of Christ. I live in a place with a full history, and complicated past, not easily understood by an outsider. It's a beautiful blend of Native, Mexican, and Anglo cultures where deep roots mixed with profound hurts shun things that are new. "Lord God," I prayed, "Give me compassion and understanding for the old things and the old ways."

As we visited the dives dotting the city, my tongue developed a love for the local cuisine. In the fall, the roasting chiles toss and turn over a fire, and the air is literally tinged with flavor. And I prayed again, "Give me a spice for life that infiltrates every corner of my being. Make it so pungent, Father, that it can't help but give you glory and attract people to you."

Every October, Albuquerque is abuzz with preparations for Balloon Fiesta, a week where hundreds of hot air balloons pepper the blue sky and hundreds of thousands of visitors come to witness the colorful spectacle. With mild temperatures, clear skies, and calm winds, Albuquerque is known as the balloon capital of the world. I find it interesting that a progressive city with its nuclear laboratories and burgeoning skyscrapers embraces an old-fashioned form of transportation. No rockets or jet packs or hover crafts. Just the rainbow stillness of floating sheets of fabric. And I petition the maker of heaven and earth to blanket my city with his perfect peace and to use our new church as a bright herald of Shalom in a dark and weary land.

A sense of place develops a love of people. By loving their home, I automatically have a connection with the people who live here. We can meet eyes over the beauty of a country and a culture. When they hurt, I hurt because their place has forged a space in my heart. The staggeringly high statistics of crime, teenage pregnancy, and the high school dropout rate break me. I can't help but want to be part of the solution by bringing the gospel of Jesus to a place I love.

LABOR PAINS

by Jodi Harris

My husband, Jeff, used to say, "I want to live and die as a youth pastor in Yucaipa, California. I can't see myself as a senior pastor." And that's when I knew God had other plans.

After an 8 1/2 year youth ministry in Southern California, God called Jeff and me to plant a church. We would begin this church in a new community just a few miles down the freeway. We wouldn't even have to move. It seemed so clear to us, and easy to me.

After all, I grew up in a church plant. My parents started a church with four other families 30 years ago, and it currently runs 1,500. How difficult could it be? In fact, my life wouldn't be affected, really. We'd live in the same house and have the same friends. I'd shop at the same grocery store and sing in the women's group I loved. My kids would grow up in this safe, small town. My faith was like Peter's. I had faith to walk on water…while I was standing in the boat.

Faithful to the Call

It was September 2000. I was six months pregnant with our second son, Benjamin, when we received the news that we would not be planting a church locally. As of December 31, Jeff's youth ministry would end. What were we to do? Initially, our faith stood strong that God would reveal His plans immediately. After all, He didn't want to stress out a pregnant woman. Pregnant women are big (no pun intended) on stability. We need comfortable homes, financial security, a freezer full of ice cream, and a due date we can count on. Of these four, I was down to one. Peanut butter chocolate was my favorite.

But God's timing was not ours; neither were His plans. As the countdown began, each day we waited on God. By mid-October, I was praying specifically for God to bring a church opportunity before November. In November, my husband and I were to fly to Northern California to interview with an area church-planting organization. I had already decided that it was too far away from our friends and family, so why interview?

My first mistake: Telling God what I did not want to do. (Or perhaps this was a good way to find out what we would be doing.) Sure enough, my husband and I flew to Northern California. While nothing was decided right away, we both came home with a sense of peace that God was moving. He would take care of us wherever He sent us.

Miraculously, I wasn't anxious. How could I not be anxious? With a new baby on the way, a toddler, a soon-to-be unemployed husband, and quite possibly a move that would uproot my family and my stable existence, certainly I had a right to be anxious. Why wasn't I? A guidance counselor told me I was in denial. Perhaps. But it sure felt good.

Perseverance Against All Logic

After Ben's birth in early December, we still had no confirmation where we would go, but I wrote a Christmas letter to family and friends stating, "If God had a womb, I'd be in it. For over the past several months, I have felt

His love and presence wrapped around our family so tightly in what could be an overly stressful time." While God had chosen not to reveal details about our new ministry yet, He chose to reveal Himself. As a postpartum mother, I had the peace that passes all understanding. So this is what it feels like, I thought.

And then January arrived, and it was not accompanied by a handbook for the Harris household for the year 2001. "This can't be right!" I complained to God. "You knew we needed a job by January 1st! How in the world will we pay our bills and feed our boys?" It was against all logic to me. Then I pictured Peter in the boat, getting ready to take a step out and walk on water toward Jesus. I'm sure that seemed logical!

"Lord, if it's You," I prayed like Peter, "tell me to come to You on the water. Tell me You have a plan to take care of us." He did. It was time to step out of the boat. For two months, we watched God provide until He would send us to our new ministry.

OBEDIENCE AND COMMITMENT

In mid-February, we learned of our church plant location in Northern California – Fremont, east of the San Francisco Bay. Two weeks later, we packed up our baby and toddler and a houseful of stuff and moved into an apartment half the size of our house, but costing three times the rent. What were we doing? Stepping out of the boat, I guess.

For six months, we planned and prayed our way through a pregnancy of a different sort. Of course, now that I think about it, I acted in a similar way: I cried daily and ate a lot of ice cream.

Our life was full of so many trials! We were doubting our call to Fremont. We had made assumptions when we stepped out of the boat, and we weren't prepared for the storms that came. When our house didn't sell and we couldn't pay our bills, we thought, "Not again!" We should have known that God would provide. Hadn't He brought us this far?

In addition, we didn't expect to be alone in our calling. We thought we would have instant friends and co-laborers for this new church. We also didn't know a tiny apartment would change our way of living and cause us to wonder if this was really worth it. All of these storms distracted us and brought doubt to our trip outside the boat. "Lord, save me!" was my sinking cry.

I had to keep returning my eyes to Jesus, and keep focusing on why we were here. God continued to strip away all of our stability and the securities of the way we had once known life. I sobbed to Jeff. "We gave up so much to do this. If I had known it would be like this, I never would have done it." How many women in labor say that?

Our 3-year-old son, Ethan, was awake in the other room and asked his daddy if he could come and give me a hug. He ran out in his jammies, hugged me, and said, "I love you, Mommy. I love you so much. I'm right here. I will take care of you. It'll be okay. Don't be sad, 'kay? We'll have fun tomorrow. We'll go to the pool, play with friends, and watch 'The Thomas the Tank Engine Show.' I'll make you feel better." God Himself reached down to comfort me through my child. He knew Ethan's touch would make His presence known. How good is my God!

Church planting wasn't about what we were going to do, but what God would do. I wasn't here to work as much as I was here to watch. Just like pregnancy, I could feel the baby move and kick and grow, but there wasn't a thing I could do but stand in total amazement of God's work.

During that time, we took a trip back to Southern California. On the drive down, we talked in detail about what the new church would look like. Blue eyes, brown hair…Oh, wrong baby!

What was our vision? Who did we want to reach? What would the service look like? Anything was possible. Over the next six months, we watched that vision come to life.

Joy Through the Trials

InRoads Christian Church became a church that meets in a coffeehouse setting. No pews, organ, or hymnals. While Jeff and I grew up in traditional churches and appreciate these elements, we realized that the lost generation of today has no attachment to them. But they find coffeehouses a comfortable atmosphere. And that is what we are hearing most people say about InRoads. "I feel comfortable here." Our church sits around coffee tables. The fellowship time is part of the service.

In addition to saying "Good morning" to each other, deeper interaction is encouraged. People are given time to discuss parts of the sermon, read Scripture out loud, or take notes on the chalkboard surface of the tables. Video clips enhance the message of the sermon. Worship is a dominant part of the service, and the Word of God is preached. We don't label ourselves as "seeker-friendly." In fact, one of our goals is to reach those who are not seeking Christ – to catch the fish who are not looking for the hook, and reel them in. Paul quotes Isaiah in Romans 10:20: *I was found by those who did not seek me; I revealed myself to those who did not ask for me.* (NIV)

InRoads also is attracting mature Christians who bring non-Christian friends not willing to enter a typical church. As we meet new people each week, we hear their stories of how InRoads is becoming part of them. We are watching God at work.

There are still storms blowing around us, but as He reaches out His hand to catch me, I hear Him ask, "You of little faith, why did you doubt?" and I want to say, "Because I ran out of ice cream!" But I take my cue from Peter and keep my mouth shut while Jesus pulls me back in the boat.

By the way–I overheard my husband say he doesn't want to church plant again. Guess what we'll be doing next?

LET'S GET REAL!

by Jen Jones

As I write this, our church plant is 7 months and 2 weeks old. To be honest, I feel like I could not be more in "it" than now. What is 'it'? The real. The junk. The messiness. The highs. The pits. The tears. The transparency. The expectations. The frustrations. "It" is the unexpected.

When my husband, Chris, and I first spoke the words 'church planting' back in 2008 we had no idea, even in dreams, that we'd be where we are. At the time, Chris was on staff at a church that just wasn't a good fit. While online one day, a Stadia church planting ad popped up. In a moment of weakness, Chris clicked the ad, filled out some info and went about his day. When he came home later that evening he told me about the pop-up and that he had expressed interest.

I immediately got excited, more excited than he. He quickly told me how it was, "Just something I did." That he, "had no intentions of it going anywhere." Reminded me that he was, "just curious."

I was a little crushed that he was just playing while I was getting very serious about the thought of moving on.

It was about a day later that Chris received a call from the head of Stadia's assessment process (CPAC). At first, Chris explained the same things he had told me. By the end of the conversation, we were picking a date to go to assessment. I was excited but I was also asking myself, "What the heck are we doing?" "What in the world is about to happen?" "Do we even know what all this means?" The answers were, "I don't know," and "Only God knows," and "Absolutely not!"

Chris and I filled out a lot of paper work. We answered a lot of intense questions regarding our childhood, our relationship with our parents and with each other, any addictions or struggles (alcohol, food, sex, porn, etc). Were there any major illnesses? So personal and deep! We tried to prepare mentally for assessment. But that's not really possible.

We got through the long, tiring, sometimes annoying process….with a thumbs up! They were very honest with us saying, "Get out a map, point, and that's were you can plant." After much prayer and discussion we chose to come to Winston-Salem, NC, which was home for Chris.

We packed up a house of four. Our kids were six and five at the time. And we moved yet again because of ministry. We spent three months with Chris' parents in their home while we looked at houses.

We settled into our home in October of 2009.

The weekend we moved into our home was also the launch weekend of Catalyst Church in Greensboro, North Carolina. Chris committed to intern 18 months with Catalyst to work along side Scott Haulter, the lead planter there.

What an experience! For 18 months, we were able to see the ins and outs, the crap and the joys, set up and tear down, fears, failures and victories!

This was, and is, the single most helpful piece of advice Chris and I could give. *Before you plant, intern!* I won't kid around, it is tough. We had to

raise our own support for a family of four for 18 months. Let's get real…
that's tough!

There are two *huge* ways Satan knows how to attack our marriages and
one of those is money.

We were asking for a beating going into that season of our life. It was
often frustrating and scary. I told Chris many times, "It might be time to
get a 9 to 5."

He kept reminding me that he was strongly convicted that we were
right where God wanted us. If he got a full time job away from Catalyst, he
would not have the same amount of time to spend with people.

Relationships wouldn't have been able to be formed. He felt very secure
in impacting the kingdom of God, continuing to do what we were doing.

After that somewhat stressful 18 months were over, we started really
preparing for our plant. By this time it was January of 2011 and we planned
on planting in Fall of 2011. We set October 2, 2011 as our official launch
date. Over the next 9 months we were very busy. Chris was buried in a pile
of paperwork and to-do lists. We were brain storming our church name,
logo, mission statement, values, colors and so on.

This was an intense time for our family. The kids were trying to adjust
to us working in our home. They were also adjusting to public school, as
was I. Our eldest had been home schooled her first two years, and our
youngest had been home until now. Our son cried everyday until
Christmas. After that, he only cried on Monday's. I'd ask myself almost
everyday, "Have we done the right thing? Was public school really the best
thing for them right now? Did I push them into a scary world too soon?"
This broke my heart!

We did all we could to comfort our children and remind them that
ministry, from here on out, would look very different then it had in the past.

We made it through the school year praising God that it was finally
over. We really amped up our game that summer. We had deadlines to
meet, lots and lots of things to purchase, fund raising, and making

connections in the community. But we also spent a lot of fun times at the pool building relationships and going on a family vacation to the beach. We had long nights watching movies and catching lightning bugs. This was a pretty good balance, but there were also far less things to do at that point.

Before we knew it, summer 2011 was over and we were back in school. Gracie was in third grade and Isaiah in first. Our kids handled it like champs this time.

When I saw the way they were now adjusted, I had peace and confirmation that we had done the right thing. That's when I had a complete realization that had we waited and put the kids in public school fall of 2011 on top of launching…we might have lost our kids.

There was no way any of us could have handled public school for the first time during a launch! Thank you, God for affirming the decision we made a year before that. Man, he always knows what he's doing! The fall came very quickly that year. Before we knew it, we were announcing our grand opening on October 2.

I need to add an important piece of information here that really changed the game for us, this was such a special time for us for many reasons. Chris' father, Jim, had been diagnosed with kidney cancer the previous fall, September 1, 2010. He had been given different answers to 'how long?' He was told anywhere from 3-6 months to 3-4 years. I had a paradigm shift at this moment. I thought our family had moved to Winston-Salem just to plant a church and try to bring people back to Jesus. It became clear that we were also here so that we could be a part of Jim's journey with cancer. Had we still been in Kentucky, I do not know how our family would have handled it. I'm not sure how Chris would have dealt with it. Thank you, God, for your provision once again!

Our broad prayer, outside of healing, was for Jim to just make each milestone here on earth. He was with us Christmas 2010, then for his 64th birthday in January, Easter, and Father's Day. But the special day we wanted Chris' mom and dad to be a part of was launch Sunday, October 2, 2011.

God blessed and they were there! There were so many emotions during launch week leading up to that one Sunday. I was beyond thrilled that Jim was able to see Chris' dream happen. Both Jim and Eleanor were supportive of us from day one. They allowed us to live with them, helped with the kids, helped do outreach events pre-launch, and also supported us financially. We thanked God that Jim was able to be physically with us on that day, strong and feeling great.

We made it through our first weeks with a small but mighty core group. During the first month after launch, I worried if anyone would come to CITYChurch . We joked because most people were just getting there as service began or a little after, so we'd start service wondering if we'd be having a gathering of just the core group...all 15 or so of us. I asked myself if our set up looked attractive. Was our flow of pipe and drape inviting? Were our people welcoming and warm? All the normal concerns that come with the first time of doing something this big! After all, our goal is to draw people into a faith community so they can encounter Jesus. If we mess that up or don't get that right, it's pretty significant. No pressure! Praise God, we made it! We made it through our first months with bumps and bruises, but we made it.

Once winter hit, Chris' father started to really feel the affects of the cancer. It was everywhere in his body from head to toe and it truly was a matter of time. Jim spent his last Christmas with the family in December 2011. He was so weak and fragile, unlike anything we'd ever seen. He had his 65th birthday the next month. He was now free to retire...from earth.

Jim entered hospice in February 2012, and spent 11 amazing days there. He talked to everyone up until the day before he passed on February 17. He would tell everyone two things, 'God is Good' and 'It is well'. To family and close friends he would say three things, 'God is good,' 'It is well,' and 'I love you.'

The emotional stress Chris was under during Jim's last months was exhausting. Chris was behind on his work due to doctor visits and appointments that he wanted to be a part of. He couldn't concentrate completely because his head and heart would wonder and worry. All while he was leading a staff and a small congregation that was a matter of months old.

I can't explain what this was like, other then overwhelming.

At seven months old, our church family found their groove, our family found its groove, and God continued to bring us messed up, broken people. I still ask myself, "Why? Why did God choose our family to lead a community in Winston-Salem? Am I even qualified? How can I be used when, at times, I feel farther from God during this process then I ever have?"

The burden, the pressure, and the time consumption of getting everything done had pulled me out of His word and away from prayer farther then I've ever been pulled. Isn't that the opposite of how it should be? No doubt, I felt guilt. These are the things I now discuss with a Christian counselor. Yes, counseling.

Next to interning, before you plant, *put counseling in your budget. You'll need it!* I don't care how strong you think your marriage is or how strong your faith is….ALL of it will be shaken and sifted in the planting process. For us, it was early on. For others it comes years down the road.

Women, seek help. Find strong Christian women that you can talk with very openly. Find one person that you can bare it all with, holding nothing back. Maybe that's a Christian counselor for you or maybe it's a best friend. I don't want to scare you too much, but it gets lonely, very lonely.

People around you don't 'get it'. I've learned you can't force them to 'get it', or make a pie chart that makes them get it. Protect your marriage, protect your children, and protect your heart from Satan. I personally feel like I failed early on at these, but praise Jehovah, his mercies are new tomorrow morning!

Women, help protect your husband. Allow him to have down time (actually make him have down time), help him plan on his calendar with family time and wife time. Discuss together boundaries of the home and boundaries of the church. Have a plan. "When _____ happens, we will do _____."

Don't get caught off guard. Don't get so caught up in 'church' that you neglect your family, spouse, and the Lord. Have a plan of action to prevent Satan from coming in and destroying these precious areas of your life.

You have made Satan irate that you would move your family across the state or county in order to bring people back to Jesus through this thing we call church planting. Believe me, there is nothing he won't do to try and stop that from happening. My experience is that he will start with you, with your home, and with your marriage. Be on guard and be prepared for the battle of your life, then go win it!

- TRANSPLANTING -
RISK AVERSION
by Melissa Hoffmeister

Many people put their money in savings bonds and money markets because they are known for steady, safe income. You don't lose much, but you don't gain much either. Being risk adverse means that you like that safe middle ground. Like me, many women love emergency funds and security, but there is little something inside us that really wants to feel emotion. We want to hit it big on that one stock, be swept off our feet to a foreign county and never have to worry about paying for new school shoes again!

I grew up with a self-employed dad. He always made sure we had what we "needed," but we never really asked for "wants" because he was working so for hard for what we had. After his long work hours, he'd make it a priority to swing by my softball game to cheer me on. Family was important to him. As I began to date, I knew I wanted a family man like my dad, but told myself I'd *never* marry an entrepreneur! In my 20s, I found myself attending college and studying Business. As much as I tried to avoid the downsides of running a company, I was drawn to the success, flexibility, and excitement it provided. There I met Brian – not an entrepreneur, but a pastor – perfect, right? Little did I know, that God was aligning our gifting for such a time as this.

For the next 10 years, Brian worked for or around church planting churches in three different states. I found myself working for Stadia, a church planting organization, as an event planner and as a recruiter for church planters. I became passionate about the need for church planting... assuming that it was "someone else's calling." I was still holding on to the security that I committed to as a child

One day, our lead pastor asked Brian and I to come into church to talk about an upcoming sermon we'd be preaching together. "I know I asked you to come in to talk about the sermon, but I really want to ask you to launch our first church plant." Both of us sat there numb. We had only been with the church for a little over a year and we were at the height of the church's success - brand new building, cushy office, generous pay and an adoring church family. We thought our kids would grow up in this town.

"You would make amazing church planters, but if you choose to stay, we'll keep you on staff." Do we remain in this life of comfort and steadiness, or do we cash it all in for hitting it big – a chance to reach hundreds of people in a city that didn't have a non-denomination church?

As risk adverse as I tried to make myself for the past 33 years, I knew what God was calling us to. Cash it all in. Go for broke. Plant a church that only He could take credit for. But it took time to let God change my heart. Our first step was to invite others to pray with us about it. Then we attended a Church Planting Assessment Center (CPAC) to see if God would speak to us through that process. He did. As we drove seven hours back home, we reflected on how God had been using the past 10 years for such a time as this.

Now we are only two months away from opening Lakepoint Church in Muskego, WI. Like the stock market, these past months have been some of the lowest points in our marriage, but these trials lay in the shadows in comparison to the extreme blessing God has poured out on our family. The leaders and servants on our launch team are more impressive than we could have ever imagined. The school district is welcoming us with open arms – even asking Brian to lead monthly leadership trainings for their top faculty. God sold our home and our staff member's homes in only four months and we were both able to purchase our next homes in the same neighborhood. With the help of Stadia, we have a planting network financially supporting us and coaching that has made the details come together so smoothly.

I'm glad my dad modeled life's highs, lows, and a strong commitment to family. As a child, I wanted an easier life for him, but as an adult, I see that the fuller life is worth it all!

The thief comes only to steal and kill and destroy; I have come that they may have life, and have it to the full. John 10:10 (NIV)

IT COULD BE ATLANTA

by Kristy Robison

"Are you sure God?" This was the question I asked many times as the Lord started wrestling with Matt and I about planting a church. "What about our children? How will they adjust to a move? We love it here, God. I have a great job that I love, we have wonderful friends and our family lives just a couple of hours away. Are you sure you want simple ol' us to plant a church?!" For many weeks, this was the dialogue I had with God. In my spirit though, I felt this tugging from the Lord, this restlessness that just kept saying, "Go!"

After much prayer and seeking the Lord, Matt and I decided to attend a church planter assessment (CPAC), to see if we were church planter material. Before I go on, I must go ahead and tell you that it has been our experience that anytime God wants us to do something *big*, we encounter a lot of opposition. This has sort of become comical in our life because if we didn't laugh, we would most certainly have to cry. This happened with our adoption journey to Ethiopia and many, many, more stories that I will have to save for another book one day.

The day had finally arrived for us to fly from Cincinnati, to Atlanta to connect with our flight to Arkansas, where we would drive to Missouri for assessment. Not too hard right? We didn't think so either, but maybe we should have prepared ourselves!

We arrived at the Cincinnati airport in plenty of time to grab a bite to eat and to make sure we didn't miss our flight. We certainly didn't want our tardiness to assessment to automatically fail us. As we sat nervously anticipating what the next few days would hold, we heard on the loud speaker, that our flight would be delayed two hours due to technical problems on the plane. Matt and I were frustrated, but knew that even with the delay, our layover was long enough in Atlanta, that we would still have no problem getting there on time.

So we waited and waited and as we waited we started noticing the clouds getting very dark outside the airport window. Our flight was delayed again until further notice due to weather. We finally got on a plane headed to Atlanta, *seven hours* after our flight was originally supposed to leave. The customer service lady assured us that we would make it to Atlanta in time to get on the last flight to Arkansas.

We arrived in Atlanta shortly before 11:00PM, when the last flight was supposed to leave. We had already missed our appointment with the counselor that was scheduled for 8PM that evening. I thought for sure we had already failed. We got to Atlanta International and ran as fast as we could to the other side of the airport. We arrived at our terminal at 11:05PM. We could see the plane sitting outside the window, but the attendant had just closed the gate. Even though Matt and I both begged to get on the plane, we had no luck and were left in the Atlanta airport with many other people who had been stranded due to the bad weather.

When we thought it couldn't get any worse…it did. We were directed to Customer Service along with a line of around 100 other people and we waited for yet another two hours for what we were told would be hotel vouchers, so we could at least get a good night's sleep. As we made our way to the front of the line at 1:30AM, we were told they were out of hotel vouchers, but they would gladly allow us to sleep in the airport to catch another flight at 8:00AM.

Then it suddenly dawned on me in that moment that *we couldn't* sleep in the airport! I had traveled many times and had *always* brought a carry-on bag with a change of clothes, toothbrush, hairbrush, make-up, etc. However, I thought this was going to be such a short trip, I had just packed everything in my suitcase which was who knows where! I could not show up to assessment already miserably late, with my hair a mess, bad breath & without my face on! There was no doubt in my mind that they would send us home right away at the sight of that! So, I convinced Matt that we needed to find a hotel room and make a trip to Walmart. It took us 30 minutes to walk across the airport since the shuttles were no longer working and as we walked outside there were mobs of people waiting for taxis and shuttle busses to take them to a hotel.

As I went from bus to bus, I was told that all the hotels around the airport were full! Are you kidding me? Now what? This is what I meant by if we didn't laugh, we would have to cry. We walked over to a rental car place, waited in line *again*, and rented a car that smelled like somebody had left a bag of rotten fish in it for weeks. We drove until we found a Super Walmart because by this time we needed it to be open all night because it was 4:00AM. We went in and I bought a hairbrush, toothbrush/toothpaste, make-up, pillow, and a blanket. We were able to sleep for two hours in the fish-smelling rental car, in a Walmart parking lot, in Atlanta, Georgia.

Matt and I agreed that our motto from this point forward would always be, "It could be worse, it could be Atlanta!" We did make our 8AM flight the next morning, rented a car in Arkansas, and got lost a few times on gravel roads where dogs were chasing us and where an owl flew into our windshield. This sounds so crazy it's almost unbelievable. There were many times on that trip that we almost called one of the core assessors, Brent Foulke, and said, "We can't do this." But we knew this was just confirmation that God had big things ahead for us. We did finally make it to assessment one whole day late, but thankfully the Lord moved and we got the green light to plant a church. But now the question was where?

When we went in for our exit interview and Tom Jones looked at us and said, "What about Atlanta?" Matt and I instantly looked at each other and burst out laughing! God does have a sense of humor. Guess where we are now? You guessed it! We planted a church right outside of Atlanta.

I can now say in hindsight, that I'm so glad that we didn't give up. I'm very thankful that God kept pressing us to keep going because if we had not, we would have missed so much that God had in store for us. The past two years have dramatically changed my life for the better. We have had very hard times where God was growing us and changing us, and so many good times where we have experienced "Church" the way we believe God intended.

We have walked with a lady who had previously been involved in gang activity, and was a runaway who had been in and out of foster care her whole life. She had tried to commit suicide three times and we watched her come to know Jesus. She now opens her home in a rough area to those that need the love of Jesus. We are getting to bring the church to people who may never come to a church building.

The Lord is moving us to "Be the church" to the homeless, the prostitutes, drug addicts, single moms, and abused and neglected children. The greatest compliment that we get is "There is something different about your church, about your people – you really love people." We may never have a lot of people come on a Sunday morning, we may never have large offerings (in fact, one Sunday we had a $120 offering), but we know we are doing what God has called us to do and that is reaching the lost and bringing them back to Him. That's really all that matters. This life is way too short to do anything else. We are not living for a reward here on earth, but for what we are storing up in heaven.

Church planting is one *wild* and *crazy* journey that you don't want to miss! Not only can you change your community, but church planting changes you. I'm not the same person that I was two years ago. I think back to that legalistic, naive, comfort driven girl that I was and I think, "Who was that person?" It is when you follow after the Lord, get out of your comfort zone, go to places you never thought you would go, spend time with people you never thought you would spend time with, open your home up to strangers – this is when transformation begins. When you love like Jesus did, you become more and more like Him. Your heart begins to break for what breaks His, you start to see people the way He sees them and as you change and are Jesus to people, slowly but surely, your community changes one person at a time.

I would encourage anybody that is thinking about planting a church to ask God, "What do you want me to do? Where do you want me to go?" Be prepared! God will move in your life and in your family's life. Put your armor on daily because you will have opposition from the enemy and you will have very hard times. To be completely honest, we have had weeks when we didn't know if we would get paid. We have had Sundays, where we have looked out and only seen a handful of people. We have had sickness and trials with our children; we even went four months without a home of our own. But the rewards are far greater than anything you could ever imagine. I could write a book about the life change that has occurred in the year that we have been a church. I could go on and on about how the Lord is moving in our community. I am so honored that God has called us to plant a church. Our family is nothing special, we are just ordinary, broken people that are loved by a perfect God, who has called us to the front lines of His mission.

For our struggle is not against flesh and blood, but against the rulers, against the authorities, against the powers of this dark world and against the spiritual forces of evil in the heavenly realms. Ephesians 6:12 (NIV)

PRUNING

prun·ing [proon·ing] *v.* **1.** to cut or lop off (twigs, branches, or roots). **2.** to cut or lop superfluous or undesired twigs, branches, or roots from; trim. **3.** to rid or clear of (anything superfluous or undesirable). **4.** to remove (anything considered superfluous or undesirable).

- PRUNING -
GOD LAUGHED
by Anne Milam

Ministry is full of unexpected, crazy and hilarious moments. You just never know what God's sense of humor is going to throw at you. While this is true of any ministry, I believe that being a mobile church lends itself to unique opportunities to enjoy divine hilarity.

One Sunday, we got a call from our volunteer who pulls the trailer full of frontline (welcome team) and children's ministry gear. Basically, the guy said the trailer was not where it was supposed to be. It was just gone!

Gone? What? How were we supposed to do nursery, preschool and elementary without any of our gear? No toys, no changing tables, no pack and plays, no rugs, no computers? How were we going to greet new people? What about all our banners and signs? What about communion? How will we do that without the trays?

Keep in mind, this was at about 7AM and our first service was getting ready to start at 9:30AM. Panic and adrenaline coursed through Dave and within minutes he had our children's minster on the line and running to

Walmart to buy whatever bare minimum items we could get, with the $500 left on our church debit card, to pull the nursery together that morning. He called all the ministry team leaders and the theater. Notifying each one of what had happened. Oh, and of course, the police. We had to call the police and fill out a report. And Dave still had to speak…to the church.

Unbelievably, it was an amazing day! Everyone shifted into overdrive and came through in creative ways. Our children's minister and her volunteers were able to put together a makeshift nursery. Our wonderful theater manager, Ernie, allowed us to view a Veggie Tale movie for our preschool and elementary kids. All the ministry teams worked together and we dipped bread into cups of grape juice for communion. Dave used the stolen trailer in his talk and our whole church worshipped God and prayed for the thieves and prayed for God to provide.

At the end of the day, we looked around at each other and felt the "peace that passes understanding," even in the midst of all that chaos. It was an event that pulled our small body of Christ together like nothing we had seen before. Effects of the stolen trailer would ripple through Kinetic during the spring and summer of 2008.

That alone would have been enough. At which point our God chuckled, because we don't serve a God of "enough." We serve a God who is able, "to do exceeding abundantly above all that we ask or think." So over the next weeks and months we saw more amazing things unfold.

Dave wanted to send a message of forgiveness to the people who had stolen the trailer. Through a connection from his sister, he was able to make contact with a local billboard company. They were looking for savvy ads to fill old billboards since advertisers were gravitating toward computerized signs. They agreed to put our billboard ads up around Charlotte for free, if they liked the look of them, we just had to pay for the materials.

Thus started the "Great Kinetic Billboard Controversy." We held a contest at church for the best ideas. What we ended up with were ads that were a little edgy, fairly humorous, and slightly irreverent, depending on who was reading them. We were a church plant after all! We could afford to take a few more risks than most established churches... especially when you have nothing to loose.

The conservative backlash in Charlotte and in blogs around the country was fairly intense. Many staunch evangelicals felt that we had gone too far. Pushed the church planting envelope beyond the limit! Parents said they had to "cover their kids eyes" as they drove down the interstate so they wouldn't read, "Church Trailer Thief: Stealing from God...Ballsy!"

Ironically, the people group our church was trying to reach, the lost, the unsaved, the unevangelized, the average nonbeliever, were not put off. They thought the boards were funny and authentic. And they started coming to our church! We had new visitors who eventually became members because of the billboards and ensuing news coverage.

And this is why God laughed, because what was intended for evil, He used for good. He makes a habit of doing that. He actually delights in it!

For your viewing pleasure, I am including some of our billboard contest ideas.

HERE ARE A FEW OF THE ONES WE USED:

CHURCH TRAILER STOLEN
Stealing from God…Ballsy

CHURCH TRAILER THIEVES:
Enjoying Our Communion Trays?

CHURCH TRAILER THIEVES:
God Forgives You – But We Need Our Stuff Back!

HERE ARE SOME OF THE ONES WE REJECTED:

These are funny to be sure, but many are definitely not appropriate for reaching others for Christ.

CHURCH TRAILER THIEVES:
We Love You Anyway. (Sorta)

CHURCH TRAILER THIEVES:
Can we have our Bibles back?

CHURCH TRAILER STOLEN
Please Return or Burn

CHURCH TRAILER THIEVES:
You just robbed God. I wouldn't worry about the cops.

CHURCH TRAILER STOLEN
Last Seen On The Highway...To Hell!

CHURCH TRAILER STOLEN
WWJD? He Wouldn't Steal From A Freaking Church!

DEAR CHURCH TRAILER THIEVES,
You're welcome. Really.

DEAR CHURCH TRAILER THIEVES,
Come see us when you've grown weary of your life of crime.

DEAR CHURCH TRAILER THIEVES:
Did you get beat up in High School?

DEAR CHURCH TRAILER THIEVES
Be careful with the snakes inside...just kidding.

- PRUNING -

CONTROL

by Vanessa Pugh

It took us a lot longer to sell our house than we had hoped. We had done so much work to our house and kept it in immaculate condition. In my naivety, I assumed that a house this well-kept would sell immediately, or in the worst case scenario three months time. Besides, God had called us to plant a church. He knew we had places to be, right? However, months passed and still no offers. I struggled with this. "God, are you seeing what's happening here? I thought you wanted us move to Cleveland? Have you overlooked this step in the equation?" I began to doubt God's plan for us.

After nine months we finally got an offer and without hesitation we accepted. We were finally on our way! We moved into the rental property next door to my husband's parents while we looked for a house to buy in Cleveland. Our kids were thrilled to be living next door to Grandma and Grandpa.

To me it seemed like it would be cut and dried. We had unloaded our house, had a nice chunk of money for a down payment on a new house and both my husband and I had exceptional credit scores. Our prospects in this new city would be endless. Which neighborhood to choose? Which house would our kids love? It made for exciting dinner time conversation.

The next four months proved to be an unbelievable test of faith for both of us and I'm afraid I didn't handle it well. We found a house that we loved and after negotiating an offer the seller decided she didn't want to move. It was very disappointing but we just trusted that God had something else for us. Then we found house number two. After agreeing on a price our realtor sat down with the seller to sign the contract when the seller had a full out melt down and started crying saying "I'm sorry, I just can't sell you my house!" I must admit, that one really shocked us. Then we found house numbers three and four on the same day. We decided to bid on our favorite house, number three, and if they didn't accept we'd just buy house number four. Well, house number three wouldn't accept our offer and house number four sold to another buyer that same day. We were absolutely devastated! I was so discouraged and began to resent God calling us to leave where we had been so happy. We decided to go on vacation with our family and start house hunting all over again a few weeks later when we got back. It was all too much to process at once

What happened next has been the most faith altering event of my life. During our time in temporary housing we had no phone, no internet and no cable. Every time I needed to send an email or balance the checkbook I had to take all of my stuff over to my in-laws shop to use the computer. It was always a major production and I was frustrated that we were still not in Cleveland. On this particular night, my 3 year old daughter begged me to let her come with me to the shop. As I was sitting at the computer, she looked out the window and saw my husband and my son playing on the swing set with Grandma and Grandpa. Immediately, she started jumping up and down asking to go outside. I was trying to finish what I was doing and with frustration in my voice I told her to just run around the front of the shop, across the parking lot and into the backyard.

She ran over to the top of the steps and while sitting at the computer I felt something nudge me. I got up and walked her down the stairs to let her out of the shop. Again, I felt something nudge me. I walked her to the corner of the parking lot and told her to run across to the house. A third time, something nudged me. I walked her across the parking lot and right as she stepped behind the garage door Grandpa started backing out. I screamed "Maddie!!" and she darted back over to me to avoid being crushed by the truck. In that moment, I heard an audible voice that said "I'm in control." I immediately started crying and hugging my daughter. My daughter could have been killed by her own Grandpa had I not responded to the nudging that kept prompting me to walk with her. God had mercy on me that day.

My entire life and my trust in God have been forever changed by that one event. I saw everything with a new perspective. I repented of my behavior and my lack of faith in God's plan and I have thanked him repeatedly for not taking my daughter's life that day. The freedom I felt surrendering everything to God was unbelievable. There are still nights I watch my daughter sleep and thank God for his mercy. I will cling to those three words as long as I live. "I'm in control."

It's amazing what God does when you give up the control and trust him with everything. I was blown away by what He did next. When we got home from vacation we resumed house hunting. We drove to Cleveland to see three potential houses. As we were standing in the kitchen of one of the houses, my husband's cell phone rang. It was a man from a real estate company calling to tell us that a deal had fallen through and our favorite house, house number three, had just come back on the market. Then he told us that the price had dropped $30,000 dollars! We put in a bid immediately and they accepted! This time we really were on our way to Cleveland.

I often look back on this whole situation and reflect on how I handled it. Ever since then I use one simple question to help myself gain perspective on any situation I'm dealing with. The question is "How do I want to be able to tell people I handled this?" It always keeps me in check.

THE TERRIBLE TWOS

by Jan Limero

Some of you might have toddlers now, others have long since survived that life stage. All my kids are well past the terrible twos, but our church more recently went through that right of passage.

The second year of our church plant was by far the hardest year of my entire life. First came the "agenda harmony" issues followed by "The Exodus". We lost about 40% of our people over a few weeks. Most had been there since pre-launch. Then, two months later, came the biggest blow of my life – my mom passed away after a ten year battle with cancer. Although I had years to prepare, it couldn't have come at a worse time. No one in our new church knew or appreciated my mom; we were reeling from The Exodus, and our small group, which had been mildly dysfunctional to begin with, was taking a "break". Following the blurry six weeks that I spent in Tennessee after the funeral, we began a long dry spell I call "Our Famine". We cratered financially as a church and therefore as a family, once going six weeks without a paycheck. Then, only six short months after my mom's death and at the height of our famine, the "C-word" came up again.

My dad was diagnosed with prostate cancer. It seemed like the wrath of the enemy was coming upon us with fury, blow after blow, month after month!

I don't tell you these things to solicit your sympathy or to scare you away from church planting, but rather to encourage you! Yes, encourage. To encourage means to 'give courage', and we all know church planting takes courage! You see, in the midst of these trying times we sometimes felt inches from being crushed. (I'm sure we all had those days as moms of two-year-olds too!) But we also felt the burning pain of our roots growing deeper and deeper, searching for life-giving water, nutrients, joy, hope. And of course, our redeemer never left our side or failed us! His Word suddenly became life-sustaining. His promises blossomed hope into our lives, like water in the desert. We ate the daily bread He provided for us, both literally and figuratively and even learned to find joy in it.

We survived the terrible twos and have come out stronger, wiser, and more courageous, just like moms of two-year-olds do. Church planting is hard work! The enemy will certainly attempt to get in his jabs and discourage or cripple you from your work. If you are going through hard times, take courage! Jesus said, "Here on earth you will have many trials and sorrows. But take heart, because I have overcome the world." Let your trails make you strong and courageous.

- PRUNING -

BAPTISM REAL ESTATE AGENT

by Holly Haulter

Maybe it was just our particular experience, but it seemed to me that pre-launch and the first few years of church planting were a constant string of crazy moments. There were many times when my husband and I looked at each other and said under our breath, "We should be writing this stuff down."

For instance, as launch was approaching, we started receiving all of our church's supplies before we got the trailer in which to store them. At one point, we had our entire sound system, projection screens, a full nursery, thousands of postcard mailers, and our brand new ice cream truck—all packed into our garage and driveway. (I'm sure the neighbors loved the ice cream truck.) In fact, one day I came home from work to find the UPS man in my house sitting at the kitchen table with my husband, looking at the computer. He had been to our house so many times that he finally asked my husband what was going on, heard about the great price my husband got on speakers, and just had to have some himself.

Speaking of the ice cream truck, driving that was also a crazy experience! We handed out free ice cream in neighborhoods and at community events; it was a wonderful tool for getting our name out there—people definitely remembered us. Having people shout out, "Hey! It's the ice cream man!" when we attended my daughter's school functions was fabulous.

If my husband's alter ego was the "ice cream man," mine was the "baptism real estate agent." Shortly after launch, a fairly eccentric lady decided she'd like to be baptized and asked if I'd help her find the perfect outdoor location. She was hoping to find a spot she connected with, that she could return to for years to come. I blindly agreed and, for two and a half hours, we drove throughout the area looking at water. Shortly after that, she told two other ladies that I was available to drive them around to find their locations. I didn't have the heart to tell them no, so each time, I agreed! On the upside, I now know every body of water in our area and the perfect places for photo ops!

The most comical experiences we've had in church-planting have come as a result of working with people who have little or no church background. We've had to change sermon series logos from "I Peter" to "1st Peter" because everyone thought it meant, "I Peter", as in "I, Robot," the Will Smith movie. We have to remind people not to bring alcohol to our church pool party and that margaritas probably shouldn't be served at small group. Our first band included several non-christians, whom we had to ask not to cuss while they practiced in another church and not to play "Grandma Got Ran Over By A Reindeer" as an opener at Christmastime. My favorite crazy moment in dealing with an unchurched person was just recently when a lady came to me after service with a concerned look and said she "had gotten coffee in her communion." After laughing, I prompted her for more info and she stated that she was sure her juice had been coffee. When we went to the man who had graciously agreed to prepare communion that month, he snickered and told us that he had run out of juice, so he decided to fill the cups with coffee. Who knows how many times he'd done that before someone was brave enough to come tell us!

Although these experiences have been embarrassing and exasperating at times, they give my husband and I joy. We recognize that each instance is evidence that we are doing something different—and that we are truly reaching people who have never known God or His Church. I know that, years from now, when I look back on this whole experience, the stress and the trials will not be what I remember the most—it will be these stories.

STORMS

storm [stawrm] *n.* **1.** a disturbance of the normal condition of the atmosphere, manifesting itself by winds of unusual force or direction. **2.** an attack or assault on persons, places, or things. **3.** a violent military assault on a fortified place, strong position, or the like. **4.** a heavy or sudden volley or discharge: a storm of criticism; a storm of bullets.

BLESSED BE YOUR NAME

by Anne Milam

One of the worst days I can remember in my church planting journey came at the very beginning of our church's launch. We hit the ground, in Charlotte, in August of 2004 with a six year old just entering Kindergarten, a three year old and a six month old. From there we began gathering a launch team of people to help us start this baby church.

In December, two months before we were due to launch, I found out I was pregnant with our fourth child. I had a nine month old I was still nursing and a husband who was stressed to the max and running around like a fiend making sure his line item planting list of 500 things was done. I was supposed to be leading ministry areas, and oh, yeah, mothering our children through this prelaunch phase. I was *so, so, so overwhelmed*. Ever been there?

I really had to hit my knees and wrestle with God on His timing here. "Can't you see how exhausted I already am? Alex didn't even get a chance to finish being a baby. And how about all the folks back home who already think we are crazy taking 3 little kids half way around the country to start some church that may not even thrive? What will they think about this? Will our adopted grandmother still even want to help us?"

I know, I know. Why was I so worried about what other people would think? Well, because I just was, and sometimes you are too, so put your stones away. This isn't even the worst part. I'm still getting to that. So after much prayer and requesting that God give me the strength and ability to bear what He obviously felt I could, I put my big girl panties on and relaxed into what had to be God's will on this pregnancy, because Dave and I certainly had nothing to do with it, well, almost nothing.

We went home that Christmas and told our families, we told our adopted grandmother, we told our friends. The reaction wasn't quite as bad as I had feared and I began to enjoy being pregnant. I actually looked forward to how this child's birth would mark the one year anniversary of our arrival in Charlotte. I made connections with other new and expecting moms and realized that God did have a plan to use this pregnancy in our little church plant!

We launched Kinetic Church at the end of February in 2005 and it was amazing. God had brought together all the loose ends and woven them into a tapestry of eclectic, beautiful, hurting people all hungry to learn about Him. So many unchurched, raw, ready to be harvested people! The beginning of the culmination of what was planted in our hearts at camp 2 years prior.

The week after Kinetic's second Sunday, we were scheduled for our second ultra-sound. Since this was my fourth pregnancy, I knew what to expect. Of course, now that I was 35, I was considered AMA. A thinly veiled attempt to suggest that I was old, since AMA stands for Advanced Maternal Age. Even though I had just had a baby a year ago under totally normal conditions, suddenly I was thrust into the "high risk" category because of a recent birthday. My doctor had told me not to worry, I wasn't any more at risk than I had been a year ago, but they do have to cover their tails and I should just enjoy the attention and extra sonograms. This sounded pretty good to me.

On a bright Monday morning, David and I trotted off to the downtown AMA office with the fancy ultra-sound equipment, our video tape in hand. Yes, don't laugh, it was video tape. As in, VHS. The hospital apparently didn't have DVD burners yet. We left the kids at home with a sitter and made a little date out of it. After all, we could show them the video when we got home.

We met the friendly ultra sound tech and she got busy splattering my 18 week prenatal-belly with ultra-sound jelly. Then she took the sonogram wand and began to push the jelly around looking for the baby. From previous experience, I remembered that they always looked for the heartbeat, they looked for the head, they looked for multiples, *Dear God, please...NO! OK, I will if it's your Will, as He gently reminded me of who was in charge,* and then they measured everything to see if size was on target for due date.

Dave and I are just hanging out in the sterile, pale room, goofy smiles on our faces as she finds the baby and points out the beautiful little head, the dark spots for eyes, all four precious limbs, tiny fingers and toes. I'm chattering away about wanting to find out the sex of the baby, if the baby cooperates, when the tech gets really quiet. I assume she is just concentrating and I keep babbling happily along about how this is our fourth baby, we are so excited, etc. etc.

Now is the "worst" part that I promised earlier. The tech quietly looks up and says unexpectedly, "If you would just wait here for a moment, I need to check with the doctor about something." Then she silently leaves the room. Dave and I stare at each other for a moment. Then my eyes begin to fill with unexpected tears and I start to freak out a little bit. The tech has never left the room before with any of our other babies. This. Can't. Be. Good. Dave is looking stressed too, but I can tell he is trying to stay calm.

After what seems like a long, long time, the AMA doctor swiftly walks in, greets us, and starts to use the wand on my belly again. Finally, he looks up and says, "I have some bad news. We can't find the baby's heart beat." I blink up at him, then at Dave, then back to the sober faced tech and ask, "Are you very, very sure? Can you please check again?" Kindly, the doctor agrees and shows us where the heart beat should be. Where a red pulse of light should be coming from the screen, there is only dark, dark grey.

He tells us that the baby is measuring maybe 15 or 16 weeks and has probably been dead for a week or two. He draws some amniotic fluid to test and instead of being a healthy, clear-ish color, I see that it is more brownish and dark. He tells us that this is from blood. We are given the choice of waiting to "spontaneously abort," sometime in the next week, or we could go ahead and schedule a D and C, or I could be induced. Such ugly, hateful words, piercing our hearts like little knives.

We decided to be induced. I wanted to see this child, to hold her and to say goodbye. Our delivery doctor was amazing. He was a Christian and shared with us that he and his wife had gone through some of the same pain. But other than that, we were alone. We were going through this huge process and no one was beside us. That was devastating.

On Wednesday morning we delivered our fourth child. A little girl. Her hands and feet were perfectly formed. Her arms and legs were amazing. Her torso a miniature of what it would have been. With a precious little head, she fit in the palms of our hands. As we prayed and cried, we marveled at how perfectly formed this child was, even at 15 weeks! All I could hear thundering in my head was, "Blessed Be Your Name, You give and take away, You give and take away, but my heart will choose to say, Lord, Blessed be Your Name." This is the song I had clung to as we left our old church and it comforted me again in that hospital room.

Little did I realize at the time that we were caught in the middle of a supernatural battle. A battle for territory. A battle for ground that would be lost or won. The enemy was crouched, leering at us, watching and waiting for us to crumble, break, retreat. Ready to take back into darkness the little inroads of light Kinetic was already making in the lives of people who were seeking God.

But our God had other plans. He always does, doesn't He? We were enfolded and lifted in prayer from all across the country. It was one of the first times I can ever say I could tangibly feel the prayer of the saints on our behalf. David and I would just lay in bed holding each other, crying and praying, but always trusting. Knowing beyond any doubt where this child was now and trusting that God was working on something. Us, our kids, our church. Something. We believed that He wouldn't waste one single tear. Not one single sorrow.

My dear friend, JJ Taylor, from college, made an unexpected and beyond generous gesture. She left her family of four children, hopped on a plane, and came to spend several days with me that first week. She grocery shopped for me, spending way more than she should have, to buy treats for us. She cooked for me, cleaned up, helped me function with my own kids. But most of all, she made me laugh again. We laughed and cried and laughed until we cried or until I wet my pants. For that sweet time of communion, I will always be grateful and can never repay.

Kinetic's third Sunday was looming and David asked if he could share what had happened to us that week with the church. There wasn't any question, of course. He had to. If this couldn't be used for God's glory, what was the point? Besides, I didn't want everyone thinking I was still pregnant and asking about the baby. This way everyone would find out at once.

But the enemy wasn't through yet. JJ and I were getting the kids ready for church and eating breakfast, sipping coffee, and talking. David had left hours earlier to help the set-up team. Chloe, my three and a half year old, had wandered into the office and was quietly climbing on a stool to look out the window. A sudden thud and a piercing scream compelled both JJ and I to jump up and run for the office. Chloe was crying and holding her little hands over her mouth. Blood was steaming down her fingers and I began freaking out, again.

I am not exactly sure what came out of my mouth as I lifted her up onto the kitchen counter to look at her teeth. I think I was asking God, "Seriously?" and maybe a few other things as well. Then I realized I would have to really calm down if I wanted Chloe to calm down and so I shifted into supernatural calm. I am pretty sure I didn't have it in myself to be that calm in that moment. But calmness came. I grabbed a towel and started dabbing at the blood. I think JJ went to get some ice. Chloe stopped crying enough to let me look in her mouth. I didn't know if she had bitten her tongue off, or bitten through her bottom lip. Maybe she had knocked all her teeth out…Oh no! She was going to be toothless for Dave's sister's wedding! A toothless flower girl!

But as I got in her mouth and looked around, I realized she had knocked her two front baby teeth down. Not sure how that had happened exactly, but they were lower than they were supposed to be and still intact. I knew just what to do. Here is where I have to give props to 11 years of experience as a youth pastor's wife. I had seen knocked out teeth before! I gently but firmly pushed her distended baby teeth back into their proper sockets. We gave her a popsicle and some Motrin and then we drove to the emergency room.

By the way, don't ever go to the emergency room for teeth. You will wait forever and then they will tell you they don't know what to do and that you will need to contact a dentist. This delightful adventure is how I found our wonderful new pediatric dentist. I called the after hours number and when she returned my call, she said I had done the right thing and to bring Chloe in the next day. Needless to say, JJ and I missed church that Sunday.

While all this transpired, Dave talked about our miscarriage during his message. The husband of a family that had been coming since our first Sunday came up and comforted Dave. He told David that he and his wife had struggled with many miscarriages while trying to get pregnant with their daughter. This man was a non-Christian. A complete skeptic and non-believer. He was a self-proclaimed believer in science and only agreed to come to church with his wife because the name "Kinetic" sounded scientific.

This was the odd man who kept wandering into the nursery to check on his child when the sermon got too intense. This was a man who, we would come to find out later, was struggling with various addictions that were tearing his marriage and life apart.

This is also a man whose family would become founding members of our church and members of our first small group at Kinetic because he felt a connection with Dave as a grieving father. This is a man whom, seven years later, God has fully redeemed.

Over the years he battled his addictions, and with Christ's help became a leader in our church. He led numerous small groups, coached small group leaders, and led others to Christ. He and his wife now have three children and recently had to move back to their home state to care for an ailing father. But his legacy, and that of his children, is changed for eternity, in part, because his heart was softened by our sorrow.

So many people comforted us with their stories during this time. I never really understood what it was like to loose a child, until it happened to me, creating real empathy in this area for others. It was during this time I realized a very private secret. Miscarriage is like a hidden epidemic. It scars so many people, but those scars are tucked away, hidden. The only way you get to see them is when you bare your scars too.

The bible promises us that every single hair on our head is counted and that every day is numbered perfectly. Don't let anyone ever convince you that a life of only 112 in utero days doesn't matter. The difference the short life of our daughter made in me, in Dave, in our family, and in our church, ripples across eternity, and she never spoke a word.

Indeed, the very hairs of your head are all numbered. Don't be afraid; you are worth more than many sparrows. Luke 12:7 (NIV)

- STORMS -

IN YOUR FACE

by Kara Simpkins

In the past, when I heard the term "spiritual warfare" I thought I had a general understanding of what that was. I thought spiritual warfare could be described as anything that tried to take our focus off Jesus and rob us of our peace. In past experiences, that came in the form of financial hardship, illness, discontentment, and an assortment of other trials familiar to most of us. I viewed spiritual warfare as something that happened from a distance.

Our family (Chad, myself, and our 3 kids) moved to Chapel Hill, NC in February of 2010 and launched Varsity Church in January of 2011. There were numerous and various roadblocks and obstacles as all church planters can attest to. We had a lack of funding, resources, people, etc. Again, normal church planting challenges that weren't too much of a surprise. We recognized this was the work of the enemy and spent a lot of time in prayer but still had no concept of what true "in your face" spiritual warfare actually was.

In September of 2011, the lease on the house we had been renting had come to an end. We had scoured Craigslist in search of a less expensive home to rent. We promised our kids that they would not have to change schools and made it a priority to find a home in our current neighborhood if at all possible. Sure enough, I found a listing on Craigslist and we set up a time to meet with the landlord and look through the prospective home. We couldn't have been more pleased. Each child could have their own bedroom, there was a home office space for Chad and I, and a big back yard complete with a play-set!

Chad and I prayed about the specific rental amount we felt comfortable offering ($300 below what they were asking) and presented our offer to the landlord. She immediately accepted and we viewed that as an "open door." We moved into our new home on October 1st.

Of course, when you are a church planting family there is no such thing as hitting the "pause" button and taking a few days to unpack and settle in. We moved in on a Saturday and I hosted my ladies small group the next Thursday morning. The group of ladies that come to my Thursday morning study are amazing. Out of the nine that regularly attend, only two would call themselves Christians. On this particular Thursday, for whatever reason, the only two that showed up were the ones that were followers of Christ.

What I am about to share with you may sound like something out of a horror movie. I have no way of explaining it away and I don't think God would want me to. If it hadn't happened to me, personally, I'm not sure I would believe it. But it happened and my eyes have now been opened to a whole other dimension of the spiritual world.

Our group was getting ready to start a new book study and because only two out of our usual nine were present, we decided to delay starting our discussion until the next week. Instead, we took our coffee, tea, and banana bread into the family room where we could relax on the couches and chit chat.

Our home is an open floor plan, with our kitchen and family room basically being one large room. Above our family room is our bonus room.

We have the Wii set up for the kids in this room and there all kinds of toys, books, and now a guinea pig named Oreo. Anyway, our bonus room is basically a glorified play room. Our four year old son, Jake, was sitting at the kitchen table playing some games on my laptop while we were talking in the family room.

About 15 minutes into our time together, I started to notice some sounds coming from our bonus room. Every house has it's own "noises" and I just figured it was the pipes creaking, the house settling, or something of that nature. I honestly didn't give it much more thought.

A few minutes later, the noises became much more apparent and it literally sounded like someone was walking around in the bonus room above us. One of the ladies yelled up, "Hey, Chad! You don't have to hide out up there. Come on down and say, 'Hi!'" I started to get *very* nervous and quickly explained to her that Chad was not home. He had gone to the local coffee shop to work. All three of us sat there in silence for a moment. Once we acknowledged the noises, they grew increasingly louder. It sounded like a 250lb man was walking around in the bonus room The floor was creaking and there were thuds that sounded like loud footsteps.

I was at a loss for words and explanations. Jake yelled out from the kitchen, "Mommy, who's upstairs right now?" The ladies and I just stared at each other in bewilderment. The warmth and peace in our home was no longer there. I felt cold and afraid and I had no idea what to do or what to say.

One of the ladies offered to go upstairs and have a look. I gave her the go ahead and she headed up our stairs. It seemed like she was up there for an eternity but it was probably just a couple of minutes. She ran back down our stairs, ran through our kitchen, and out our back door!

I couldn't make myself look at her or the expression on her face. I felt completely paralyzed by fear. After a few seconds, my brave friend came back inside. She said that she couldn't explain it, but there was some sort of dark presence in our bonus room. She was visibly shaken and said she was ready to leave.

Yeah, me too!

I closed our group with a quick prayer, thanked the ladies for not totally freaking out, and assured them that Chad and I would get to the bottom of this. I sent them both out through the front door, grabbed Jake and my phone, and ran out the back door. I told him to play on the play-set for a few minutes while I called Chad.

Poor Chad, he must have thought that I had been attacked (in a sense, I was). I completely lost my composure as soon as I heard his voice. I explained what happened and begged him to pack up and head home to protect us from who knows what.

Chad was home in less than five minutes. As Jake and I remained outside, I saw Chad through the window, baseball bat in one hand (for physical protection) and his Bible in the other hand (for spiritual protection). Chad said the house felt cold and strange to him, too. He said it was difficult to physically make himself read from the Psalms out loud. He started at the bottom of the staircase and worked his way up the stairway, his voice becoming bolder and louder with each step.

After a few minutes, he came outside and said it was safe for us to come back in the house. I was hesitant. But sure enough, the fear and coldness that I had experienced earlier had vanished. First lesson learned, The Word of God is a powerful weapon!

We were all three still shaken and decided going out for lunch might be a good idea. We never let Jake know what was going on by the way. He seemed pretty oblivious and we did our best to change the subject and down play the whole experience whenever he asked about who was upstairs in bonus room We told him it was probably our dog making all that noise (impossible, our dog is only 13 lbs). Someday, at the appropriate time, we will tell him what really happened.

Chad and I decided that we needed to take a crash course in spiritual warfare, ASAP! He spent the afternoon sending out an email to his management team and trusted advisors asking if anyone had ever experienced anything similar. In an attempt to educate myself, I got online and googled "spiritual warfare."

Between the two of us we had numerous conversations that day and came to the following conclusions:

1 We were NOT crazy!

2 There is a spiritual world around us that exists whether we choose to be aware of it or not.

3 This type of thing is not totally uncommon, especially when Satan is feeling threatened.

4 WE DONT HAVE TO BE AFRAID, THERE ARE WAYS TO FIGHT BACK AND RECLAIM OUR PEACE!

The next morning, a dear friend of ours (and fellow church planter) came over to our house to pray over our home with us. One of the ladies from my group watched Jake. We went through each room, anointing each window sill and door frame with oil. While in each room, we took turns praying scripture, asking for the Lord's presence to reside with us and claiming His protection and blessing to be upon us.

We included every room, even the attic space, the yard, the garage, and especially the *bonus room*! In all, we spent about an hour and a half in prayer. I wasn't sure what to expect and was pretty anxious about the whole thing, especially when it came time to pray over the bonus room area.

Let me assure you that all I felt was *peace*.

Warm, quiet, reassuring peace.

"In your face" spiritual warfare is real. I hope and pray that I will never encounter anything like that again. But, if and when I do, I am confident in my new found arsenal of weapons. In the face of darkness, I don't have feel powerless or overcome by fear. I can and will fight back.

When we speak the name of Jesus, fear and darkness have no choice but to disappear! Praying with confidence and reading scripture out loud are great defenses as well.

The lesson we learned is, no matter how busy and hectic life is, we will always take time to pray over any home our family lives in. We recommend you do, too!

SPIRITUAL WARFARE

by Jennifer Fillenger

Spiritual warfare. It takes a certain amount of bravery to even write those words.

So often, I like to pretend that I am not under attack by dark forces that want to shut us down and make us go away. We get attacked often enough that I can't pretend it isn't happening. Sometimes it's almost funny…almost.

Some days his ploys are so obvious and yet they can completely take you off-track. For example, right as summer break began I decided to drive over to the park to exercise. On a one-way street, a car backs up into me. As I am reaching into my van to get a pen to write down his information, a huge tour bus nearly takes my door off.

The driver of the tour bus was sweet as pie until the New Orleans Police Department (NOPD) officer came and then he started lying, saying that the wind had caught my door and that he had clearance until then. No citations were issued at the time because the officer cited wind as the cause.

That officer's supervisor saw the report a week later and decided to cite me for having my door open in traffic, because you can't cite the wind.

I spent four weeks getting my van fixed and fighting the citation, which would put me on the hook for the ticket and both of our deductibles. It was discouraging and insanely inconvenient, especially when I am the only one jumping through hoops and I was the one who got hit. Twice.

Then God came through.

On the bus behind the one that hit me was the Dean of LSU's Medical School and his trusty iPhone. I got to know him pretty well in the hour we waited for the NOPD to arrive and he gave me his card. I e-mailed him requesting any pictures he took of the accident and lo and behold, there was no wind! There is a flag drooping from a flagpole right above us.

Also, the driver could have been over an additional 3 feet according to the shadow of the bus behind it. My flashers were on, proving the tour bus was coming up to an accident scene. I have proof and my insurance is fighting it.

It was an amazingly well executed attack. My nerves were shaken, we were without our car, my integrity had been questioned and my husband and I were edgy with each other. He didn't understand what had happened until he saw the photo. We must be on our guard against Satan's attacks. Don't get me wrong, to focus only on that is to fail to believe God is big enough to win, but Satan hates to lose. Think about it, if you knew you were ultimately going to lose the war, wouldn't you want to take down as many committed, advancing front-line soldiers as you could?

Church planters are advancing soldiers.

Whose ground are we taking?

That's right. And he is not happy about it.

Take it anyway.

EMBRACE THE TENSION

by Sondra Rush

I am not sure that anyone can ever be totally prepared for what God has in store for them. I know that I wasn't. I never anticipated that I would be where I am now. On so many levels, I am forever changed as I choose to follow after such a gracious and faithful God. This whole church planting venture has been one of the hardest, yet one of the most rewarding things I could have ever chosen to say yes to. It is something that continues to draw me closer to Jesus, and continues to challenge me all at the same time.

It is somewhat difficult to share all the ways in which this church planting journey has challenged me. Something I can tell you is that it has been a love/hate relationship. I love that more than ever, I am learning who God is, who he says I am, and how, out of response to that, I am learning to live my life. I love that my husband and I are closer, on all levels, than I could have ever possibly imagined. I love that my kids get to live in a diverse and broken city, where they can see their parents trying to live a life out of response to the gospel message, to their neighbors, and everyone else around them. Striving to love people where they are, because Jesus loves me where I am.

Yet, the strange part about all of this is that all the things I love about my church planting journey, have grown out of most of the things I have struggled with. Within the first year of moving to Lakewood, Ohio, in Greater Cleveland, where we felt God calling us to, we have experienced as much heartache as we have joy. We have seen as much damage and darkness as we have restoration and light. So many times I have felt like we are fighting a battle we are unequipped to win, and that is the truth. Even so, I am also learning that this is the very reason why we need and cling to Jesus. When you are living out the mission of God, things will get messy. The only thing that can redeem the mess is the power of the gospel message.

Let me explain. When you move to a new city, you already have some adjusting to go through. But when you move to a new city to start a new church community, you are overwhelmed on a whole other level.

Within the first year of living in Lakewood we have experienced...

- Reoccurring (and often completely unrelated) illnesses. The week we moved into our new home my two daughters, a three year old and a one year old, had double ear infections and conjunctivitis that lasted for weeks. My husband, soon after, had to be taken to the hospital and was treated for pneumonia, gastritis, and double ear infections. During all of that, I was three months pregnant and just trying to stay afloat.

- A bedbug infestation in the other apartment of the duplex we lived in. Talk about paranoia! Although we never got them, I still itch when I think about it.

- Learning to rely on God to provide for both, our mortgage payment from where we moved from and the rent for our place in Lakewood. Each month we were never completely sure where all the money would come from.

- Someone who was on trial for the abuse of his infant son joined the launch team and for months tried to hide it from the team. When my husband confronted him on his lack of transparency, he began attacking my husband and his leadership. We felt the pull of Satan trying to tear apart things even before we launched.

- One month after we launched I gave birth to my amazing daughter, Mylah. The day I brought her home from the hospital, our neighbor, a single mom with two kids of her own, had a homeless family of four move in with her. Considering that this neighbor lived above us, it sounded like a herd of elephants were living there. Needless to say, sleep was at a minimum.

- Learning to love the GLBT community beyond reason, even when it was awkward. One Sunday during setup, before our worship gathering, a first time guest who was transgender 'accidentally' fell into my husband and grabbed his butt. Twice.

- On Sunday morning, New Year's Day 2012, we woke up to find out that our church trailer got broken into, and $7,500 worth of equipment was stolen. Happy New Year!

- A first time guest of our church came and told me that someone must have been smoking an organic substance in the bathroom of the middle school we gather in for worship. And I'm not talking about buckeye leaves. How's that for first impressions?

- Eight months after launch my husband and I awoke to a sinking feeling that *we are all alone in this*. That we were the only two people who *really* cared about the mission God has called us to. As we gave way to these feelings, anxiety set in.

When these sort of things happen to you, you may want to pack up and turn around. You may want to say, "All right God, I have had enough." But the tension that comes from our broken world, is the same tension God uses to restore it's broken nature. I sometimes describe it as that place where I feel the pull of this world and my human nature, against the pull of the Kingdom of God at the exact same moment.

Paul describes it best in 2 Corinthians 12:9-10 when he states, *"But he said to me, "My grace is sufficient for you, for my power is made perfect in weakness. Therefore I will boast all the more gladly about my weaknesses, so that Christ's power may rest on me. That is why, for Christ's sake, I delight in weaknesses, in insults, in hardships, in persecutions, in difficulties. For when I am weak, then I am strong."*

I think this bible passage explains it well. It explains that when you go through junk like bedbugs, illness, and all the other dark and broken things of this world, that if you choose to trust God, then he will redeem all of it. It is out of those dark places that God and his gospel light will shine the greatest, and you will be stronger, and better for it!

One of my favorite Florence in the Machine's song says, "I am ready to suffer and I am ready to hope!" I feel like I hate the suffering, but I am now at a place where I would follow Jesus into the darkness, the ugly places of this world. Even if that means there is going to be hardship, I'm ready to hope. I am at a place where I am learning to let go of control. Learning to love those who are different and far from God. Learning to trust God with increasingly more of my life. This is what the gospel does. It enters in and gives hope to the everyday hopelessness of the world. The pre-chorus of the same song says, "It's always darkest before the dawn" and it is becoming the pre-chorus of redemption for my soul and my city.

Below is a poem I wrote about the tension in the middle of this crazy church planting journey. In the hard times may it encourage you to know you are not alone, and that God will use it if you let him.

What is it with tension?
Always around the corner, waiting to sneak up and paralyze you.

I truly have a love-hate relationship with you tension.
You get in the way, and yet you push me to grow.
How do you always know where to push and pull,
and sometimes suffocate me in the very place I needed it the most?

Lately I have been wrestling with myself,
Questioning my abilities and allowing fear and pride to get in the way.
Somehow, there is always a self-inflicted tension that creeps up on me when I am
trying to follow Jesus.

And it is in those moments that I am learning to pray for courage and strength.
Because doing the opposite leaves me all alone-
Misplaced.
And my innate reaction is to run and hide,
waiting for some magical concoction to make it all collide
Come together and make some sense,
you know, without the Tension...
Oh, how I wish!

That tension is the place that has something to do with our broken world that is waiting. Waiting to be restored by God's wreck-less love. Waiting for the arrival of our liberating King! Tension is living in the in-between; choosing, watching and waiting for the Kingdom to break in.

Embrace the tension.

WAGING BATTLE

by Vanessa Bush

My eyes open abruptly and my hands rummage blindly on my nightstand for my phone. Only 2:30AM. Outside I hear the wind talking. It rushes across the open mesa with no trees or buildings to block it, and I know I hear voices in it as it pounds on the windows. I don't want to shut my eyes again because the nightmares will return. The accusations will begin again. "You aren't good enough. You can't do this. Don't you remember the terrible things you've done in the past? Do you really think God could use you? Get over yourself."

My husband tosses restlessly beside me. I wonder if he's having that dream again, the one where he's weighed down by something heavy on his chest, so weighed down he can't move, can't run. I hear a little boy's anxious cry, "Mommy!" coming from across the hall. This is how it happens in our house. No one is exempt from a spiritual attack. Even the two-year-old dreams dark, and the black lab turns three times in her crate, like she does, rattling the metal lock. When I see our worship leader the next day, I see it in his eyes too. No sleep for him either. Sometimes I feel scared to ask people to join our team knowing they will experience it too.

Albuquerque boasts over 310 days of sunshine per year, but never has this intense anxiety struck every member of our family during the day. No, fear strikes in the shadows. And that's just where we've moved our family. To a land lurking with shadows parading as light. In our hometown, the warfare came in the way of busyness and greed and distraction, but in New Mexico, the evil is palpable because people here believe in it. Native American spiritualism and a hybrid Mexican Catholic religious superstition permeate the culture. We who are trying to spread the message of Jesus are met at every spiritual intersection with fear and doubt. In a single week, a person may attend our church gathering and then go meditate in a sweat lodge to obtain a more intense spiritual experience. Another may come to New City, but then not feel as if their dose of holiness has been sufficient and so head to mass to perform the familiar rites. Ancient beliefs and rituals are rooted deeply.

We can count on a collision with darkness every time good is on the horizon for our little church. It's just as rhythmic and sure as the native drum beat. When we help the poor or host a big event, we must dig our heels in and prepare. We must know that he is who is with us is bigger than he who is in the world. I spend extra time praying over curly heads nestled in bunk beds asking God to spare them the fear. I pray for peace over anxiety and courage over doubt. Oddly enough, on those nights that end in a crowded couch and circles under my eyes, I have peace. The evil one cannot touch us. He wants to scare us because we are threat to his old, old system that has worked for so long. It must mean God has given us the platform and the vision to intimidate these evil principalities. When we say yes to church planting, we say yes to that challenge.

WEEDING

weed-ing [weed·ing] *v.* **1.** to free from weeds or troublesome plants; root out weeds from: to weed a garden. **2.** to remove as being undesirable, inefficient, or superfluous: to weed out inexperienced players. **3.** to rid something of undesirable or superfluous elements.

THE HIGH PRICE OF BARGAINS

by Jan Limero

I love the thrill of finding a good bargain. That's why I like garage sales so much. I love paying pennies on the dollar for what the retail price of an item was. I feel like I have gotten something for less than it is worth. It makes it hard to ever buy something new and pay the price on the tag. That price seems so arbitrary and inflated. It's not really "worth" that much, is it?

But as much as I love a bargain, it bothers me when I hear people say that salvation is free. It makes it seem like something you find in those "free" boxes at garage sales. It's thrown in with the stained shirts and Tupperware lids that have no container. Sure, I do nothing to "earn" it, but it's not worth very much either. That's not how it really is with the Kingdom of God. We might not have to earn this treasure that is far more valuable than old Tupperware, but there is actually quite a high cost to the Kingdom.

The "cost" to the Kingdom, unlike an inflated price tag, is something I actually like to pay. It's like the "cost" of a good hike. Last fall I hiked to the top of Half Dome and, believe me, there was a great cost to that hike, even though I didn't have to pay an entrance fee for the trail.

But that is the kind of price that I love to pay. I think we were actually made to pay that kind of cost. It feels good to conquer, to breathe deeply, to use all your lungs and muscles and will power to make it to the top. If you drive the paved road to the top of the mountain, the short cut may seem like a bargain, but it's just not the same. Sure you get there cheaper and easier, without cost to your muscles and joints, but you miss out on the priceless journey.

Church planting is not the place for bargains either. There certainly are mountain top experiences, but there are few short cuts to those great vistas. That's ok. Those journeys to the top, usually through the dark cold valleys, are where the adventure is. There is no glory in a paved flat path. You don't remember and talk about those kind of hikes, "remember when we took that paved path to the top?"

It's the "high priced" trips that go down in history and will be told by your children—the trips you conquered valiantly. Ask my kids about my blister/romance story, or about the time we almost all got hypothermia and ended up in a closed ranger station bathroom making hot chocolate on our camp stove to warm up and stay out of the wind. My kids know them, even though they weren't there. Those are the stories you love to tell over and over, the ones with blood, sweat, tears and near death experiences.

I'm sure you have your own harrowing church planting stories; the times you weren't sure you would make it, or weren't sure if you wanted to make it, or the stories when you were trapped in fog and all of a sudden God's light shone through. Ah yes, that is the beauty of church planting. Those are the stories that we have the privilege of living and telling! Don't fear them or avoid them. Embrace who you are, where you are and how you've gotten there. I'm sure it hasn't been a bargain trip. But I'll bet it has been worth every bit of the cost!

"For I know the plans I have for you," says the LORD. "They are plans for good and not for disaster…" Jer 29:11

DAD, YOU ROCK!

by Debbie Jones

We were a typical family in ministry just like you. We had decided to leave the comforts of a traditional church and move our family to Centerville, Ohio to start a new church. We had two children, Melanie and Tom and a cocker spaniel named Dixie. Our minds and hearts were racing with excitement as we had visions of hundreds (ok…maybe even thousands) coming to know the Lord through this new church. Every week our family drove to a local elementary school to set up for Sunday Service. Of course this started out fun, but after time this task seemed to be less and less appealing. With schedules becoming more and more demanding, it seemed hard to carve out precious time just for our family. Every day seemed to be consumed with ministry so Tom and I decided we would make a family fun decision and purchase a season pass to Kings Island amusement park! Whooo hoo…what a great decision that was! We even created a signal, just for the *Jones Family* that would let our kids know that after church service we were headed once again to our favorite get-away….Kings Island! A wink of the eye meant it was a Kings Island Day!

The kids now loved setting up and tearing down the church as they spotted us winking back and forth. Tom would even give a quick wink in a sermon just to remind the kids, a special family day was coming!

This was a normal Sunday and we were all excited that the "special signal" had been spotted several times during the morning. We drove home from church, pulled into the driveway, ran up the stairs to change clothes when suddenly, it all came to a screeching halt with the sound of the doorbell.

As I opened the door, there stood a woman with a suitcase in her hand saying "I left him…yes, I left him today!" I wanted to say, "How about leaving him tomorrow? We have family plans today!" but of course, I hugged her and welcomed her into our home. There glaring down the steps, were our two kids, knowing that today's special plans were now in jeopardy. Tom looked at me and said "Honey, you and the kids go ahead and get in the van."

A few minutes later Tom joined us, started the van, and off we went. Of course, you're wondering what happened to this woman in crisis? We wondered too and this was a defining moment for our family. Tom said, "I've taken care of finding a safe place for her and will work with her tomorrow. Her situation is not going to be able to be fixed in one day. But today is *Kings Island day* for our family!" As you can imagine, the kids were yelling, "You rock Dad….you're the best Dad!"

From that day on, we knew that our family was Tom's number one priority. It was a defining moment for us as we drove to have special time together. Not church time….but family time. Tom was passionate about helping people, but he was also passionate about his family! We saw his heart for us that day loud and clear.

Starting a church was one of the best decisions we ever made for our family. So much of who our kids have grown up to be today is because of their wonderful experiences in the church. However, setting boundaries is critical and letting your family know they are number one, is essential. I pray that you will find a place to step away from hectic schedules. Taking time for your family is one of the most important examples you can give your new church. Don't apologize or feel guilty to love your family. I'm sure glad Tom made our family a priority years ago and still does today. I pray you too will hear the words, "You rock, Dad or Mom!" as you join this incredible journey of starting a new church.

PAPER PLATES
ARE OKAY

by Vanessa Bush

For me a crowded home creates a satisfied heart. Some of my most treasured memories include people accepting Christ at my dinner table and relationships forming on my couch, not to mention a church starting in my living room. I love my house to be the party house, but I can so easily fall prey to Pinterest perfectionism. I must constantly remind my inner Martha that every meal does not require a hand-stitched table runner or homemade luminaries or even made-from-scratch food. Being a church planter's wife and having a houseful of people go hand-in-hand. But it's easy to make hospitality all about me.

Hospitality is not the same as entertaining.

Entertaining is prideful. It says, "Look at my decorating skills and culinary expertise. Aren't I great?" But hospitality focuses on our guests and their needs. Is their need a place to stay? A listening ear? Companionship? A comfortable haven from the storm of life?

When we practice this others-focused hospitality, we get to live the gospel. Jesus put all of humanity's needs above his own when he died in our place. And like him, we should be in the background when we have people in our homes and place our guests in the foreground. Humility makes hospitality happen. It's not about showing off or simply sharing a meal; it's about showing love and sharing life.

Seven practical tips that have helped me stay focused in my hospitality.

1 Create margins because busyness is the enemy of hospitality. We must go beyond politeness and intentionally seek after people. If we just wait for hospitality to happen, it won't. I try to remember that hospitality is not part of what I do; it's part of who I am.

2 Keep up with housework so that you are not frantically cleaning before people arrive. We have had evenings where I'm yelling at the kids over the vacuum cleaner to pick up their things. Clearly this is not going to create the most pleasant environment for my guests because everyone is frazzled before they arrive.

3 If you have a two-story house, I've found it's fairly easy to keep downstairs relatively neat to allow for people to drop by. Of course, the upstairs can be completely trashed and no one is the wiser. I'm always amazed at how at ease Jesus was with interruptions. He let the little children come to him and healed the woman of her bleeding disorder all while on his way to do other really important things. I want to be available like he was.

4 Leave small gifts for overnight guests. I scribble out a quick welcome note and leave some water bottles and pre-packaged snacks.

5 Host holiday orphans at your place. We've cleared out our furniture and put up folding tables in order to make room for huge crowds for Easter, Thanksgiving, and Christmas dinners. Military families, college students, empty nesters, and people who can't afford to fly home bring a dish to share and celebrate with new-found friends.

6 When we purchase new furniture or other items, we do so with hospitality in mind. What will wear well? What will be comfortable for our guests? What will be fun for our guests? For Christmas we asked for a big family gift of an Xbox Kinect from my in-laws. Now some evenings are spent with friends laughing over Just Dance.

7 Freeze meals. We try to have people over for dinner often, so I triple or quadruple recipes to make a few pans of meals I deem company worthy. Then I won't have to cook the next time we have someone over. You can also use a freezer meal to take to someone who's had a baby, surgery, or a death in the family.

My favorite company dinner is below. Enjoy!

Chicken Stuffed Shells with Spinach Cream Sauce

One box large pasta shells

Cook pasta shells in boiling, salted water until barely cooked. Drain. Let stand in a bowl of cool water until ready to use.

Filling:

3 tablespoons butter
3 teaspoons shallots, chopped fine (yellow or white onion works too)
1 cup mushrooms, chopped
3 slices prosciutto, chopped fine (I've used bacon before in place of prosciutto.)
2 cups cooked chicken, shredded
2 tablespoons parsley, chopped
15 ounces Ricotta cheese
1 egg, beaten
¼ cup grated Parmesan cheese

For the filling, heat the butter in a medium skillet; add the shallots and mushrooms; sauté until tender, about 10 minutes. Add the prosciutto; sauté 2 minutes. Stir in chicken and parsley. In a large bowl combine the Ricotta, egg, and Parmesan. Fold in chicken mixture until blended. Set aside.

SAUCE

3 tablespoons butter
3 teaspoons all purpose flour
2 cups milk, heated
10 ounces, frozen chopped spinach, drained and squeezed dry
1 teaspoon lemon juice
1 teaspoon salt
pinch of nutmeg
freshly ground pepper
¼ cup Parmesan cheese for topping

For the sauce, heat the butter in a small saucepan; gradually stir in flour. Cook stirring constantly until smooth, about three minutes. Gradually stir in milk and cook stirring constantly until smooth and thickened, about 10 minutes. Puree the spinach with the cream sauce in a food processor. You will probably have to do it in two batches. Add the lemon juice, salt, nutmeg, and pepper. Set aside.

Preheat oven to 350 degrees. Lightly butter a 9 x 13-inch baking dish. Drain and dry the pasta. Fill shells with the chicken mixture. Arrange in the baking dish. Pour the spinach cream sauce over top. Sprinkle with some Parmesan.

Cover with foil and bake 30 minutes. Uncover and bake until browned and bubbly, about 15 minutes. Let stand approximately 10 minutes before serving.

This can be made ahead. I fill the shells and pour the sauce and put a couple pans in the freezer. Then just defrost and cook when you need a quick meal.

- WEEDING -

SOILS

by Jennifer Fillenger

"A farmer went out to sow his seed. As he was scattering the seed, some fell along the path, and the birds came and ate it up. Some fell on rocky places, where it did not have much soil. It sprang up quickly, because the soil was shallow. But when the sun came up, the plants were scorched, and they withered because they had no root. Other seed fell among thorns, which grew up and choked the plants. Still other seed fell on good soil, where it produced a crop—a hundred, sixty or thirty times what was sown. Whoever has ears, let them hear." Matthew 13:3-9

30, 60 or 100 times what was sown.

I teach math, so I gotta do the numbers for a minute. There are four types of soil here: along the path, rocky and shallow, thorny and good. So, if we are being optimistic here, we have about a 25% chance at success in winning any particular person to Christ in a lasting and life-changing way, under the pulling marbles out of a bag premise. I do grant-writing on the side and they say a good grant-writer will get 1 in 4 proposals funded, so I can tell you first-hand, that 75% rejection saps your energy and pummels the optimism out of you.

Looking at it as a story problem, it is pretty cut and dried; not everybody is going to come to the party. It doesn't take long before those soils have faces. These bad soils represent people who you spend hours in anguish praying with and for, people who return to their abusive husbands or their addictions instead of trusting God, people who don't want accountability or truth in their lives and people that you care about deeply. They each turn away from God's mercy, or maybe just from your sweet little church, for one reason or another and it is utterly heartbreaking.

When we do achieve success for God's glory, it has various yields. 30, 60 and 100 times what was sown are all huge blessings. This verse was a gift for me, because in New Orleans we are tilling some pretty hard soil. God's reminder that a yield of 30 times what was sown is amazing, and that has allowed me to wish those blessed with 60 or 100 times what was sown, well. Here there are lots of birds, rocks, thorns and sun and precious little good soil. When people do come to Jesus, they are more broken and hurt than I have ever experienced. Perhaps it is the added anguish of Hurricane Katrina, perhaps it is because the pits are deep here and they are celebrated. There is no shame in this culture for things that would embarrass folks most other places. Some days it can feel like it's not even worth scattering seed.

Then you hit good soil.

We distributed something like 60,000 postcards and got a grand total of two roommates to visit our little church plant. But those two girls, once they felt the love of Christ's community and grace at Hope Church, brought 9 friends, who started bringing their friends and family. Both our worship leader and youth leader, whom we hired from within, are directly attributable to those two girls. So were our postcards 'successful'?

One household out of 60,000 would tell you no, but the response of that one household changed the very fabric of who we are. We were diverse before, but now we are younger and more musically talented by far and we have an amazing youth group led by a good friend of theirs. If those girls wouldn't be here without the effort and expense of those post cards, then it was unequivocally worth it.

You can't look at someone and know they are your good soil. There is a couple here now that I prayed would move back from California to help us (Katrina forced them out). They moved back, in fact they live not 6 blocks from where I sit, but they decided to help a struggling church plant across town.

We had an incredibly rational, intellectual Taiwanese girl visit that asked particularly pointed questions after her first service. I wasn't sure if we'd see her again, ever, yet she hasn't missed a week of Life Group or Worship Service since. She plays violin and guitar in our band and invites her friends and family to join her. If you had asked me two years ago which of these two would have made the most profound impact on our community, I would have gotten it dead wrong.

So, scatter seeds and don't try to figure out who God will use to grow your church plant for His glory. Allow the Holy Spirit to guide you in how much time and effort you put into any one seed before determining whether it is good soil. Be willing to accept that someone who you care about may not be good soil right now. God knows that the DNA must be right in our church plants from the start and He knows just what kind of garden we are supposed to be.

FOR SUCH A TIME AS THIS

by Gay Idle

Do you ever just stop and look back over the tapestry of your life? Looking back on the tough trials, the new challenges, the surprising changes that have taken place in your life…trials, challenges, and changes that at the time seem to have no rhyme or reason and think, "What the heck was *that* about?" I have come to realization that many of those times, those unexpected paths God had led me down, were in preparation for the season to come. This lesson really hit home when God led me down the road of becoming a church planter's wife.

The first years of a church plant can be the most challenging for the planter's wife. Many jobs need to be filled in order to just get the church services and ministries up and running. If you were a "parachute drop", as my husband and I were, the responsibility of setting up each ministry within your church sits squarely on your shoulder's, until God brings along someone else who is capable of taking over. I was certainly no exception to this, as I found myself taking on many roles and responsibilities for which I had absolutely no passion.

For me that role, you know, *the one for which I had no passion*, was the children's ministry. At the time we began the church plant, my passions revolved around three areas: women's ministry, music (vocal teaching and coaching), and my family. I felt that setting up and implementing a Children's Ministry with passion and purpose was a real stretch for me!

But as I began to pray for direction, *and another person to take over*, God did something pretty amazing. He put within my heart a new vision. This vision was for every volunteer in our children's ministry to understand that we were not there to babysit children, but to partner with their parents in their children's Biblical education.

I began to realize that God had actually already prepared me for this role many years before, partly through my own experience in simply raising my own children, both who were now adults. I knew what it was to raise children in "the nurture and admonition of the Lord," my passion being to make sure my children were raised to see the world around them through the lens of scripture so that as they began to form their own views and opinions they would not be drawn away from God and enticed by the world around them, but remain grounded in a faith that had become their own.

Okay, now I was excited about this vision! I saw myself in a broader role, not the one in the nursery or the children's church area every Sunday, but one who would lay the groundwork for a ministry that would one day be turned over to the person whom God would call. I began to see another way in which God had already prepared me for the task at hand.

Around eight years ago, my husband and I were pastoring a church in Florida. I had been teaching music part-time for the private christian school affiliated with the church, while also teaching at a local college as an adjunct voice instructor. Although the church had a christian preschool as well, I had no interest doing music for the preschool. I liked working with older students.

My comfortable world was thrown in to a bit of a whirlwind when the preschool lost its director and the school board asked if I would consider taking over. This was not an easy task. My education was in music education, primarily vocal music. Taking over the director's position would require six credit hours in early childhood development and childcare management, and other classes required by State.

I did all of this while taking on the position with a provisional license. Amazingly, I found that I loved working with the teachers and the parents of the preschool. I found that this ministry became precious to me as I was allowed the privilege of speaking Christ into the lives of many young mothers. I thought that perhaps this was the purpose of my being a preschool director. I know that God did use me through this position in ways I would have never dreamed possible.

At that time, I thought that this director gig was just one of those side roads we take at times on the journey to our true purpose. Now I can now see that in God's economy, nothing is wasted. I was more than prepared when it came down to the nitty-gritty tasks of setting up the children's ministry: picking age appropriate curriculum, knowing the necessity of background checking, and many more details.

I was prepared because God had taken me completely out of my comfort zone years before and placed me in a position that I would have never chosen for myself! I was prepared because He instilled in me a vision. A vision that could never have come from within myself, only from God...and because I recognized where the vision originated I can only give Him all the glory!

Our church plant, Journey Community Church, is nearing its third anniversary as I write this. I was just recently given the privilege of turning the children's ministry over to our newly hired associate minister, and yes, I breathed a sigh of relief as I handed it over. You see, I know that this was not a position that God had called me to for the rest of my life, just for a season, in the words of Mordecai, "for such a time as this."

So I want to encourage you to take up the mantle that God has placed upon you, whatever that may be, knowing that God will use all of it for His glory and good pleasure. It may only be for a season. But I promise you that you will one day look back on this season in fondness; with wonder and gratitude as you ponder all God has done with all that you surrendered to Him.

SEEDLINGS

seed·ling [seed-ling] *n.* **1.** a plant or tree grown from a seed. **2.** a tree not yet three feet high. **3.** any young plant, especially one grown in a nursery.

PROGENY'S PROGRESS

by Anne Milam

If there is one thing every church planting mother is concerned about, it's the affect of church planting on her children. Moving cross country and into new territory, leaving schools, doctors, friends and church family all create stress and disrupt our kids lives. Add to that the fact that both parents will be heavily involved in getting a new church started from the ground up, without a familiar network of caregivers, and a mother's anxiety is bound to skyrocket!

I don't know about you, but I think motherhood is the litmus test by which I will judge the success of my life. I had many jobs before I was a mother and I daresay I will have many more after. But the one job that I will always consider as my life's work, is how I raised my children. With all of that on the line, it's sometimes easy to forget that God loves our children even more than we do. They are, after all, His children first. We are only privileged to be allowed to spend our lives in the role of parent. Ultimately, it is our hope to stand side by side with them on streets of gold, as brothers and sisters in Christ.

With this end in mind, we must trust that God wants what is best for our children. He wants them to choose Christ's salvation as much as we do. His path for them may be a totally different journey than the path He chose for us to come to know Him. This can be frightening for us as parents because we know what worked for us, and we want guarantees. But there aren't any guarantees, are there?

We can only be faithful in our calling as parents and partners with Christ and trust God with the rest. We have to remember that faithfulness begins at home. If our children see us constantly putting the church and other people's needs before them, they will start to resent the church and ultimately God.

While we are busy making disciples in our new churches, we can't forget that the most important people we are called to disciple are living right in our homes. Discipling our children is a sacred opportunity. If we save the whole world, but our children loose the faith, what have we accomplished? We will have failed to pass the baton and will have missed the mark.

Finishing this race well will require us to make wise choices. Our churches need to see us put our families first and we, as pastors, need to set the bar high on what balanced family life looks like. Even if balls drop at church. Even if people get angry with us. Even if it makes some unhappy.

My kids have learned more about loving the church at Kinetic than I think they would have anywhere else. My two eldest children serve in ministry areas that would probably be filled in larger churches. They are learning to love the church by serving her faithfully and finding their place.

When we left Indiana, they told everyone we were moving to tell people about Jesus. Our mission was their mission.

THAT'S A GIFT

by Jennifer Fillenger

What happens when you drag your kids across the country (or out of country) on a mission from God to plant a church?

Well, I am so glad you asked!

Mine got funnier and more confident and flexible. They got to decide who they were in this new place and version 2.0 turned out to be pretty cool. In fact, my younger son is on version 4.0 already, with some newfound girl attention in his post-glasses phase (Ah, the power of contacts!).

My older son is articulate and well spoken and has impeccable comic timing. Both of them have tried things that they would have been shy about back in Ohio: art, drama, sports, music lessons. They are more fluid and adventuresome. They have thrived in this process of living out their faith.

I worried at first about keeping kids overnight who couldn't go home because of addiction and/or abuse or having a family friend sleep on our couch until she could get into detox. I fretted that their innocence would be lost or they would become jaded in some deep recesses of their souls, but you know what? It wasn't like that at all!

Do you know how to get your kids to appreciate you?

Show them a mom coming down from a half-gallon a day vodka addiction.

Do you know how to get them to stop whining about what they don't have?

Bring a kid over that marvels at how good they have it.

When your kids are actively engaged in their faith, God is real to them in a way no sermon can teach. Think about it; which is more meaningful? A message about the great commission or following God's plan in your life to plant a church? Obviously saying, "Here am I, send me," and then actually going somewhere is going to have the greater impact.

Our story is a little different from many planters in that my boys got to buy into the vision for New Orleans early on seeing Katrina refugees in the Super Dome and on rooftops. The need for grace and order and compassion and love here was palpable. They immediately got why we had to go do something about it. The vision aspect may be a harder sell for some than others. If you have little ones, that is best of all. They won't even know this isn't normal! Kids, at least mine, come with this innate distorted view that easy=good and hard=bad. Nothing will break them of that fallacy faster than church planting.

Is it hard? Uh, yeah!

Is it beautiful and rewarding and meaningful? Oh, yeah.

Now, not everybody will have the same experience we did. Some of it depends on the kid. Introverts will have a harder time at first. The whole new school/new church/new house thing is daunting to anybody at first, but it takes some character and chutzpah to show the world who you are.

Everybody should have a time in their life to be new and different, to explore who they are and who they strive to be. Giving them that opportunity along with a healthy family life and a Savior worth emulating, well, that's a gift.

PARTNERS IN THE GOSPEL

by Vanessa Bush

My oldest son's kindergarten Spring Break occurred during the first year of our church plant. In order to avoid the inevitable complaint of, "I'm bored," some of the neighborhood ladies and I decided to band together. So with our group of six-year-old boys and their younger siblings in tow, we headed out of town up to a cabin in the mountains where little boys could sword fight with sticks and throw pinecone grenades to their heart's content. It was the perfect plan. Moms on the porch, feet up and a cold drink in hand, enjoying the view. Little boys in the dirt, shoes off and army men in hand, relishing their freedom from a desk.

None of these other moms were Christians. They knew why my family and I had moved to New Mexico and what we were doing. I could see they were baffled sometimes because I didn't fit their stereotype of what a Christian, much less a pastor's wife, should be. I didn't pray at all hours of the day or sing the praises of the Republican Party. I didn't even have a Jesus fish on my minivan, much less a school of tiny fish following my big one. And I wore cute shoes. Church planting wives can wear cute shoes, by the way.

For some reason, these women who are worldly and lovely embrace me, and I love them back, not with a motive, not simply so they will come to church. I care for them because we laugh and cry together, because their pasts are beautifully interesting, because our children are hilarious together, because of their quick wit and goofy banter, because I see God's image in their eyes.

But spending time with these families means preparing my children privately. The little one is too young to understand, but my oldest, with his keen observational skills and his daddy's interpersonal instincts, he sees the differences. And so I explain. They don't know Jesus, so the things that are important to us are not important to them. "They don't know who Jesus is!" My first-born is shocked. He can't remember a time in his short life without Jesus. But he understands that God has made them our friends so we can show them and tell them who Jesus is. This makes sense to his little rational self.

Together he and I have been memorizing Philippians 2. Verse 5 has been particularly helpful with discipline. During our mountain excursion somewhere between fighting off an imaginary tree dragon and hunting for buried treasure, that strangely resembled rocks, my sweet boy started to act out. I went over to reprimand. "Micah, what should your attitude be like?" He responded contritely, "My attitude should be the same as Christ Jesus." I hear another small voice pop up from behind the woodpile. "Christ Jesus, who's that?"

Before I even had time to respond, my six-year-old was sharing the gospel with his buddy. After he finished his mini sermon, he looked knowingly at me, and I smiled at him. My son and I were partners in the gospel. I watched his camouflage Crocs scamper across the pine needles knowing that this boy whom I had carried in my womb, he and I were on mission together.

BLOSSOMING

blossom [**blos**-*uh* m] *n* **1.** the flower or flowers of a plant, esp conspicuous flowers producing edible fruit **2.** the time or period of flowering (esp in the phrases in blossom, in full blossom) — *vb* **3.** to develop or come to a promising stage: *youth had blossomed into maturity.*

- BLOSSOMING -

EVERYTHING IN COMMON

by Holly Haulter

Amidst the daily stressors of starting a new church, God occasionally sprinkles in little reminders of how the role of church-planters is unlike any other ministry position—and how blessed we are to be part of it.

When our church was approximately one year old, we had the honor of sharing the Gospel with a family from Suriname, South America (parents & two young boys). They were raised Muslim, but after a few months of attending our church, they joined a connection group and were baptized. Despite pursuing U.S. citizenship for many years, they received notification that they would soon be deported back to their third-world country. Multiple attorneys became involved; it was a tedious ordeal and everyone agreed the chances of winning their case were slim. All along, the family asked the church family to pray, but their connection group did so much more. They contacted congressmen, held fundraisers, and wrote letters to the judge. Then, they had a far-fetched idea: Suppose the connection group was to establish a college fund for one of the boys, with the condition that he must graduate from a U.S. high school to receive it. While it was obviously an attempt to manipulate the system, perhaps it would convince the judge that their church family was willing to put their wallets where their mouths were to keep them in the States.

Unbelievably, those eight families committed over $9,000 to the fund! That, alone, was incredible. But, then it became a work of God. In the courtroom that day, the judge announced that his own sister had been in the Peace Corps and had been stationed in Suriname. He recalled her account of the devastating conditions and determined that these children could never receive a reasonable education in such an environment... especially given the generous college fund that had been established! They won their case that day and will receive their green cards shortly after—they are now eligible for citizenship. Praise God!

I was so proud of our little Body of Christ that day! It reminded me of the early Church in Acts 2:42-47, "they had everything in common. Selling their possessions and goods, they gave to anyone as he had need." That group sacrificed in a way I've never seen any other church family do.

As leaders of church plants, we often attract people who've never been part of any church before—people without "expectations," who are simply on fire for Jesus and for their new church family. Conversely, we also attract long-time Christians looking for something more authentic, personal, and radical than they've experienced in the past. When these people converge in a brand-new church, they are so exciting to be around! Instead of being stale or jaded, they're optimistic, eager, and passionate. As leaders of new churches, we have the unique opportunity to form their impressions of what church should be—to point to Jesus and the Early Church and say, from the beginning, that is how we should love one another. And, when you finally get the opportunity to see it lived-out, it makes all of the struggles of church-planting totally worth it.

A MONSTER LURKING

by Jan Limero

About a year into our church plant, we realized there was a huge monster glaring at us. It was quite a challenge to keep from walking in fear with this monster lurking in the shadows. It was big; big enough to devour us as a church. It was a financial monster.

When we finally got a good look at this monster's face, it sent us running to God. Our board of directors called a fast before we came together to discuss how to defeat this thing. We realized that there were many practical things we needed to do in the physical world to get things on the right track. But the scariest thing that God told us to do had its roots in the spiritual world, even though it would be played out in the physical. God told us that in order to have, we needed to give.

We had just taught our congregation:

"Bring all the tithes into the storehouse so there will be enough food in my Temple. If you do," says the Lord Almighty, "I will open the windows of heaven for you. I will pour out a blessing so great you won't have enough room to take it in! Try it! Let me prove it to you! Malachi 3:10

Now God was asking us to model it for them. Even though our church checking account had $0, we had money in the bank, set aside as a church planting fund, a tithe, from our own church start-up money. Now, in our time of need, this money, $10,000, was calling out to us, tempting us to use it for the wrong purposes, for our own benefit – to pay bills, rather than to start new churches. God was now asking us to go in the opposite direction of trusting in our money, to the direction of giving our money away generously as an act of trusting God to supply all of our needs.

This money was set aside to help start our first daughter church. But that was not a reality on the near horizon. Besides, generosity is about sacrificial giving. God asked us to give away our $10,000 church planting fund to a new Stadia church plant a few hours away. They had encountered obstacle after obstacle. They could greatly benefit from our giving.

Do not withhold good from those who deserve it when it's in your power to help them. If you can help your neighbor now, don't say, "Come back tomorrow, and then I'll help you."
Prov 3:27-28

I would love to tell you that we obeyed immediately, full of faith and anticipation of God's goodness. But, we hesitated and delayed in fear. My husband, David, and I had not had a paycheck for a month and our mortgage was due in days. Unless God did something *big* we were not going to be able to pay our bills as a church, and we personally would miss our mortgage payment.

We found ourselves huddled back together as a board of directors asking what to do now. The more we looked at the church planting money, the more it called to us. But now it was calling to be given away. We realized that we hadn't had enough faith. We finally decided we would go the distance and drain the last money we had as a church. We wrote a check to the new church as an act of putting our trust in God and not in our money.

Don't store up treasures here on earth, where they can be eaten by moths and get rusty, and where thieves break in and steal. Store your treasures in heaven, where they will never become moth-eaten or rusty and where they will be safe from thieves. Matthew 6:19-20

And then we waited...

The arrow shot up, up into the air and out of sight...

Faith is the step between promise and assurance. Every miracle large or small begins with an act of obedience. We may not see the solution until we take the first step of faith. -unknown

We breathed a sigh of relief just knowing that it was out of our hands now, no longer in our power. It is a freeing place to surrender completely to God. Your spiritual muscles stop fighting and striving and fall limp into the arms of your Savior, the one who was meant to save you in the first place.

Strengthen ye the weak hands, and confirm the feeble knees. 4Say to them that are of a fearful heart, Be strong, fear not: behold, your God will come [...]; he will come and save you. Isaiah 35:3

Of course, our God came! The very day that our home mortgage payment was due, someone gave the church a check for exactly $10,000! He had heard our story and was inspired by the Spirit to replace the money we had given away in faith. It was to go into our general fund to pay bills and payroll.

Songs of joy and victory are sung in the camp of the godly. The strong right arm of the Lord has done glorious things! Ps 118:15

The arrow hit the monster dead on. Even though our financial troubles didn't end in one day or month. I believe this was the deathblow to the monster that eventually took its last breath. It began in faith and ended in victory.

The church planting journey is full of monsters. It takes faith and courage to follow His voice and His plan to defeat them. Don't discount the hard things He calls you to do. He asks you to take the narrow road, but...

My God shall supply all your needs according to his riches in glory by Christ Jesus. Philippians 4:19

RAISING OUR BABIES

by Vanessa Bush

I became a mom for the third time a month ago. And even though we had done it all before—the quickening and the growing and the anticipating and the birthing—it was just as miraculous as the first time. And for me it was more memorable, knowing this would be the last time I would carry a little life inside me.

Evangeline, our own little piece of good news, was born strong on a Friday. It was windy outside when she came into this world with an alert peacefulness neither of her older brothers possessed. They were born groggy. But this one, finally my girl, she and I stared at each other and took each other in for her first minutes on this planet. After all those months of waiting I could finally take in her sweet face and cuddle her tiny body.

And just like with my other babies, the responsibility of raising this precious soul feels like the weight of the universe pressing in all around me. How can an imperfect person like me direct a child in the way she should go without the intervention of the One Who Is Perfect?

In the midst of our family's sweet miracle, our church plant goes on. And isn't church planting so much like parenting? We worry, we work, we delight, and we mourn. Can't the weightiness of our churches, all those souls, feel like bricks on our chests, especially in our weakest moments? My temptation is to do more, go earlier, stay later, give more, sign up more. My temptation is to say, "I cannot possibly do this church planting thing. I am not good enough. It is just too big." Are those your temptations too? I read Isaiah 49:15 recently.

"Can a woman forget her nursing child, that she should have no compassion on the son of her womb? Even these may forget, yet I will not forget you."

Oh, sweet relief. God loves our churches more than we do . . . because they belong to Him, not us. I am enthralled with my newborn; I can't stop kissing her chunky cheeks and examining her tiny fingers. And God sees our churches, and each dear person in our churches, in that same way—as a mother sees her baby. I can trust that He holds my church in His hand, and that He is in control of it.

- BLOSSOMING -
LIMINALITY
by Jennifer Fillenger

Liminality.

Funky, English major word, I know, but if I had to encapsulate church planting in one word, that would be it. Liminality is choosing to step across a threshold with humility and obedience toward an unknown, but longed for, end. It is giving up the former way of life for a greater purpose. That in-between time where someone proves his or her character and convictions is liminal time. The entire trilogy of Lord of the Rings is liminality in action.

Who will go?

Only a brave and noble few stepped forward to go on the great quest to save Middle Earth. You, my friend, are on a brave and noble quest to save your city, but you have an advantage the fellowship did not; your supernatural guidance comes not from a white wizard but from the God of the universe Himself. We get glimpses of the importance God places on challenging ourselves for His sake in James 1:2-4.

Consider it pure joy, my brothers, whenever you face trials of many kinds, because you know that the testing of your faith develops perseverance. Perseverance must finish its work so that you may be mature and complete, not lacking anything.

There is no growth without challenge; God's word revisits that theme time and again. It is in pursuing His purposes that we achieve life that's truly alive. It is in this time of testing that we truly learn to lean on God, because what other choice is there? We are seeking to do something beyond ourselves- with us it is impossible, but not with God. Every part of our lives will be challenged and tested…our marriage, our patience, our integrity, our faith…and that can be so good. When you work together for a higher purpose, you are bonded in a way unimaginable prior to your quest. Be forewarned; your experience as a church planter will change you. Remember at the end of *Lord of the Rings* when the Sam, Frodo, Pip and Merry went home to the shire and it all seemed so simple and they realized how much they had changed? You will be changed- it's up to you whether it is for the better or not. You can reap a harvest of perseverance and maturity or pride and bitterness. I love that God gives us a charge like Aragorn at the end of I Corinthians:

Be on your guard; stand firm in the faith; be courageous; be strong.
Do everything in love.

Does that not sound like a battle cry? Are they not words that could be called out while astride a mighty steed? Something in us wants to be used for noble service. We desire to be called to a something greater. We yearn for purpose and meaning. Our souls resonate with Isaiah's. When the Lord asks "Whom shall I send? And who will go for us?" we, too, want to say, "Here am I. Send me!"

INFLUENCE

by Janet McMahon

WILL YOU RESIST OR WILL YOU EMBRACE?

I've always done it. I have always resisted responsibility. From the time I was old enough to babysit, I remember not wanting to be responsible for someone else's children. And then I became a mom…whew! Really? I am responsible for this little person? I mean when you become a mom the buck stops here. If you can't comfort this crying little "bundle of joy" who can? Yikes. I cried the day my mom left after visiting on the occasion of the birth of my first child. I knew that once she left, and my husband went back to work, I would be totally responsible for this baby. I was sure I was not equipped to do this!

I was frustrated and a bit angry with the world. I mean really…*they* just let anyone go out and get pregnant? Seriously? There should be some strict rules about this, some guidelines. You have to have a license to drive a car and yet *they* let anyone go and have a baby. What is wrong with this world? I was downright mad. Mad at my husband for wanting this child, mad at my parents who could have warned me the weight of the responsibility that I would undergo.

I fretted and stewed and woke up in a cold sweat…oh no, that wasn't sweat…that was milk leaking out of me. For crying out loud. What was this all about? Not only was I the only mom this child would have, I was uniquely qualified to feed it. All this baby had to do was cry and milk started flowing. Weirdest thing I have ever experienced. I spent a few months completely and utterly resisting the responsibility of parenting.

Then one night, after about 4 months of total lack of sleep and exhaustion, it happened. Probably around 2am. The crying started, the milk was ready, the husband snored, leaving me to take full responsibility. I begrudgingly drug myself out of bed to feed the child. I sat in the rocker, the moon shining brightly through the open window, and then it happened. True joy. True peace. And I began to experience a sense of purpose, responsibility and an understanding of my influence in the life of this child. I actually felt grateful. I was incredibly glad that this was my responsibility and only mine. No one else could do it…just me. I was uniquely qualified and prepared for and called to be the mom to this baby. It was a God ordained moment.

I wish I could say from this moment on I embraced my responsibility and influence, that I never again complained that others weren't doing their part. But I can't say that. Truthfully, there were still moments where I just wanted to cry and say, "This isn't fair, what have I got myself into, I have ruined my life!" But even though those moments still came, my 2AM experience was a turning point. I began to embrace my responsibility and influence in the life of this child. Even on the hard days, I celebrated my calling as a mother and I saw it for the blessing and privilege that it is.

WITH GREAT PRIVILEGE COMES GREAT RESPONSIBILITY

My favorite movie of all time is *Ever After* with Drew Barrymore. A remake of the Cinderella story, Drew Barrymore plays Nicole (Cinderella).

After her father dies, Nicole's stepmother takes away all of her privileges as an heir of her father and turns her into the house maid. Through a series of movie-like circumstances, Nicole ends up meeting the Prince. As they are getting the know one another and the prince is complaining about his privileged life, Nicole says to him, "with great privilege comes great responsibility.

Dear church planter wife. You are privileged. Really, I mean it. Before you roll your eyes, before you think I don't know what your life is like, or how hard it has been for you lately, listen to this truth....you are privileged. Are you feeling that way today? Or have you forgotten that in the hurts and hang-ups of the church planting life? Whether you haven't yet ever recognized your role as a privilege, or whether it felt like a privilege in the early days, but not so much today, I believe it is true.

Here is what I believe. Your husband loves Jesus. (Cause Jesus is the only reason anyone in their right mind would ever, ever plant a church, right?) Your husband is trading his life to help people find and follow Christ. Your husband is a gifted leader. Your husband is a dreamer. He is motivated. He is a hard worker and a make-it-happen kind of guy. He believes. He has a calling. And this gifted, talented, leader, preacher, apostle, chose you to walk this journey of life with him. Yes Ma'am you are the lucky one. Do you ever have that moment? Sunday morning, you watch him teaching the people up front. Saying things he is not smart enough to say on his own, being all anointed-like. And you say to yourself, "Girl, I had sex with him last night! Oh yeah, I'm the lucky one."

Maybe you want him, but you don't really want church planting. Or maybe you wanted church planting when you expected the journey to be more fun, successful, fulfilling, glamorous, or.....you fill in the blank. In any case, currently wanting it or not, God picked you. He placed you right where you are; married to the man you are married to because He has a plan. And you have a choice. You can resist or you can embrace the calling, the privilege, the responsibility and the influence.

Check out what Paul says in Acts. 17:26, *"From one man he made every nation of men, that they should inhabit the whole earth; and he determined the times set for them and the exact places where they should live."*

God has been working throughout history creating and placing people in a historical moment in just the exact place where he wants them to be. I am convinced that when we are obediently following Jesus, and we listen and hear from God we are where we are and we are who we are for such a time as this.

Remember the story of Esther? She did not necessarily choose to be living in the royal palace, she really did not even choose to marry the king of Persia and become Queen. God uniquely placed her there. Through an evil plot of the king's advisor, the Israelite people, Esther's people, were going to die at the hand of the King. Esther is encouraged to risk her own life and intervene on behalf of her people. She hesitates. And her cousin Mordecai says these words, *"For if you remain silent at this time, relief and deliverance for the Jews will arise from another place, but you and your father's family will perish. And who knows but that you have come to a royal position for such a time as this."* Esther 4:14.

Esther was given a position of privilege. She didn't necessarily choose it, but is was a position of privilege none the less. And with that privilege came responsibility, an opportunity to use her influence as Queen for the good of the people. Look closely at the words of Mordecai here. He says, *if you remain silent at this time…deliverance for the Jews will arise from another place.* In other words, Esther, God is going to save His chosen people. He will find a way. He doesn't need you to do it. But, He will use you to do it, if you choose to embrace your influence.

Friends, as church planting wives, God has given us a position of privilege. And with that privilege comes comes influence.

INFLUENCE – GOD'S TOOL IN YOUR HAND

Hold on! Wait just a minute here you say. I am no Esther! Well, here's the funny thing. Esther was no Esther either. She waffled. She considered wimping out. But then Mordecai reminded her that the fate of the people did not rest on her. Instead, God was inviting her to play a part in the grand rescue He was orchestrating for His beloved people. That perspective changed the game for Esther. She suddenly wanted to play, even if it meant putting her life at risk.

God called Esther to a play a part. A big part. But he didn't leave her without tools. He gave her the tool of influence. And she used it at just the right time to accomplish God's great plans.

I became a church planters wife in 1998 when my husband left his career as an engineer to become a pastor and church planter. Ummm…yes, I freaked out. We had been married for 10 years at the time and I didn't really see it coming. He was going to make half of what he was currently making as a successful engineer for General Mills. We had two kids and a mortgage. *And* he was going to have to raise half of the half of what he was going to be making….urrrgh.

But after the dust had settled and I cried for 24 hours straight, I knew that God had clearly called my husband, and I encouraged him to step into this role. My husband started the second campus of Community Christian Church in Romeoville, IL. And Community Christian Church became multi-site before multi-site was cool.

I didn't think much about being a church planters wife really. I just kept doing what I was doing serving in the church in the ways that God had called me to serve. It's funny, I remember saying to Community Christian Church's lead pastor's wife, Sue Ferguson, my very good friend, that she had influence. I remember telling her once that because she was married to Dave, she just automatically had influence. What she said mattered, it mattered to me and it mattered to others. She listened politely because she is a great friend. But as a look back I can see how telling someone they have influence because of who they are married to, can be… well…offensive.

Here's the deal. On my worst days, I don't really want to have influence. I just want to run from responsibility and hide in my introverted corner. On my best days, I want to make a huge impact on the world. I want God to use me in a way that makes an eternal difference in the lives of others. And I realize that it is very hard to make a difference in the lives of others unless God gives me some tools; one of these crucial tools is influence. BUT, I want influence because of ME, not because of my husband, right? At the core I am selfish and life and ministry is all about me. So when I am operating in that selfish place, it offends me if you tell me that I have influence because I am the wife of a pastor. I want you to tell me I have influence because I am a great leader, teacher and evangelist. Here's the tricky part. Influence is influence…either way, it is not something I get to own, it is given to me by God. So when I lay down the selfishness, I am grateful for any influence that God has allowed me to have because it has the potential to make a difference in the lives of others.

You can run from it, pretend like we don't have it, pass it off as not significant….but none of that changes the reality. The truth. When you are married to a pastor, a leader, you carry influence. Like it or not, want it or not…it's there. You can make it grow or you can suppress it. You can deny it or you can acknowledge it. You can resist it or you can embrace it. Friends, when we choose to embrace it, influence becomes a tool. A special tool given to you by God to be used in His grand plan to rescue his beloved people.

INFLUENCE FOR GOOD OR FOR EVIL

In 2007, God sent our family to Kansas City, Missouri to plant Restore Community Church. Leaving Community Christian was one of the hardest things I have ever done. Those people, that place, this church, had changed the entire course of my life.

I could relate to Paul in Acts 21:1, as he was leaving the Ephesian elders to go on to Jerusalem, it says, *"After we had torn ourselves away from them..."*

Can you relate? Of course you can, you are a church planter. God tears us away, only to begin something new and amazing somewhere else.

In any case, it really wasn't until we moved to Kansas City to begin Restore that God began to talk to me about my influence. Funny, I had thought about Sue's influence, but not my own. Here is how it went down. We were busy working in the community, casting vision for this new church. Thanks to Community Christian, we had a bit of a clue on what we were doing. Many who joined our launch team were seasoned Christ Followers who were eager to see a new Church plant in Kansas City, but had never planted a church that was designed to help people far from God find their way back to Him.

So some of what we shared sounded intriguing, but a bit unfamiliar. Sometimes they would hear stuff from Troy and then they would come to me and ask this question in various forms. Is this *really* how we are going to do it? In that moment, the vision was on the line. What I would say next mattered. I could say something like, "No, of course not, that is just one of Troy's crazy ideas, once we get started, he will get more realistic." Or I could say, "Yes, I have seen this vision bear fruit before and I believe that it will help many find Jesus right here in Kansas city."

See the difference? Oh, I was tempted to say the former. Because after all, I wanted to put their mind at ease, help them feel comfortable, but even more honestly, I wanted to say anything I could that would make them stay with us. Can you relate? In those early days, every single person that decides to be on mission with you is like gold. It makes me think of Paul's words, *"I thank my God every time I remember you. In all my prayers for all of you, I always pray with joy because of your partnership in the gospel from the first day until now, being confident of this, that he who began a good work in you will carry it on to completion until the day of Christ Jesus."* Philippian's 1:3-6

In any case, what I said mattered in that moment. I could support the mission or water it down, I could motivate and inspire or perpetuate a lack of faith in what God was going to do. I had a choice, and what I said mattered because God has given me the tool of influence. Believe it friends.

And then this happened. Someone new in the church comes to me and asks me about someone else in the church. You know, so and so? Well so and so is just not the right person for this or that. I think he or she is too this or that. Blah, blah, blah... Again, I have influence. I can build up or I can tear down. I can say, I have seen these positive qualities in this person and I am confident that God brought them to Restore for a special purpose and reason. Or I can say, "Yeah, I noticed those qualities about so and so and it drives me crazy too!" Both statements would be true. So and so does drive me crazy. But is it also true that God brought them to Restore for a reason, even if that reason is to help me grow in grace, mercy and patience?

Anything not good is evil. Sorry. It had to be said. Anytime we are not putting God or others first, we are operating in an evil place that has the potential to interrupt the mission of God. Now you could argue that if I make a few missteps in my conversations with others (and I have made and will make more than just a "few"), that it is not evil, it is just a mistake. But here is what I am coming to understand. Anything that is not loving to God or not loving to others is sin and sin separates me from God, and anything that separates me from God is evil. Matthew makes no apologies about calling us evil, *"If you then, though you are evil...."* Matthew 7:11.

When I make missteps in my conversations with others, I am usually operating out of selfishness, fear or anger. All of which are evil places.

BUT WAIT, THERE'S HOPE!

"Make a tree good and its fruit will be good, or make a tree bad and its fruit will be bad, for a tree is recognized by its fruit. You brood of vipers, how can you who are evil say anything good? For the mouth speaks what the heart is full of. A good man brings good things out of the good stored up in him, and an evil man

126

brings evil things out of the evil stored up in him. But I tell you that everyone will have to give account on the day of judgment for every empty word they have spoken. For by your words you will be acquitted, and by your words you will be condemned. Matthew 12:34-36

Because of Jesus, we can be made good. We can be a good tree, planted by streams of water, yielding fruit in season. (Psalm 1:3). We can bring life, refreshment, grace, peace and hope to our community. We can be like a refreshing drink of water for our husbands, our children and our church. We can bring positivity and faith to every situation. Our words can build up and help people believe in God's great plans for our community. We can help people understand that God has gifted them for service and tell them all the good gifts we see in them.

My church planting friends, since we have influence, we better be seriously praying for wisdom. *"For this reason, since the day we heard about you, we have not stopped praying for you and asking God to fill you with the knowledge of his will through all spiritual wisdom and understanding."* Colossians 1:9

We can wisely use the gift of influence that we have been given to bless the world!

GARDNER'S NOTES

note [noht] *n.* **1.** a brief record of something written down to assist the memory or for future reference. **2.** an explanatory or critical comment, or a reference to some authority quoted, appended to a passage in a book or the like: a note on the origin of the phrase. **3.** a brief written or printed statement giving particulars or information.

HINDSIGHT IS 20/20

by Anne Milam

This chapter is all about what we wish we could change and what we are glad we did. Compiled from a poll of church planting wives all across the country, this list is some of the best advice in a nut shell. These planter's churches range in age from prelaunch phase to twelve year old church plants. Each drop of advice here was hard won in many bloody battles. It is shared lovingly by these women, from their hearts to yours. This is where you'll hear tragic or hilarious advice and hopefully you can learn from our mistakes!

THINGS I WISH WE HADN'T DONE:

1 I wish we had cultivated a "mother" church. If at all possible, avoid being what is called a "Parachute Drop" church plant. This is where your family is dropped off in a city and told, "Here's some money. Go plant a church, somewhere, somehow, with somebody, good luck!" Alright, maybe it isn't this bad, but almost. You are usually relocated to a city where you know no one and have no connections. You literally have to start from scratch.

Sometimes this type of plant is unavoidable, but if at all possible, try to partner with a sister church who can help send you out and provide you with a launch team of mature believers and givers. I'm not saying you can't make this type of plant work, you will survive. It's just really, really *hard!*

2 I wish we had asked close friends to come with us. If at all possible, don't go alone! Ask people to go with you. Be bold, be unafraid, and ask. After all, you are doing what God has called you to, right? Find people you love and who love you, and ask them to partner with you. It's possible you may get all "no's" for an answer. But you just may end up with the best launch team ever. Look around at people who do life with you. Ask faithful friends at your church if they would be willing to go on this glorious adventure with you and come plant a new church.

Here is what one planter said, "I wish, I wish, I wish, we had done that more aggressively. Oh sure, we made a general announcement that if anyone wanted to come with us, we would love to partner with them. But we didn't sit down, one on one, with our friends and petition them to join us in this Kingdom work. We had this failed belief that God was calling us to this hard thing, but surely we weren't supposed to ask others to enter this hardship with us? What kind of friends would we be? Well, what kind of friends were we to allow them to miss all God's glory on this faith building journey?"

There is nothing more powerful and amazing than doing church planting with people you love and who love you back. Together your families are pushing back darkness to bring the kingdom of God to a new city. Share it with someone if you can.

3 I wish we had not been so afraid to fire a bad hire in the beginning, when we knew it wasn't right.

4 I wish I hadn't tried to do too much. I spread myself too thin and everything got a 30% effort. Nothing was done well! Weigh your priorities, trust God and empower others to do other things that must be done.

5 I wish I hadn't put my health last. I wish I would have paid more attention to my physical and mental and emotional health needs. You are NOT super human.

6 I wish I had prayed every night with my husband for our church and for our family's protection.

7 I wish my husband had been able to have someone to mentor him and pour into him more during pre-launch and even post launch. And me too!

8 I wish I had scheduled some extended Sabbath rest. Avoid exhaustion and burnout by putting 2-3 quiet retreats on the calendar to reflect and recharge.

9 I wish I had guarded my personal time with Jesus as my number one task for the plant.

10 I wish I had trusted God more and not worried.

11 I wish I had supported my husband by not looking at things that weren't getting done around the house, but loved him better by making his day as good as I possibly could as a ministry to him.

12 I wish we had not parachute planted and I wish I had let go of doing so much.

13 I wished we had laughed more and played more.

14 I wish I had encouraged my husband more, and spoken words to build him up.

15 Delegate, delegate, delegate! I wish I had delegated more. Pick what is really important.

16 I wish I hadn't worried about what everyone was thinking. Everyone is not going to love you or your husband. Don't people please.

17 I wish I'd cultivated close friendships as a priority. Instead, I called long time friends as I was losing it early on. My poor friends didn't get much from me the first couple of years. I needed more than they had to give.

18 I wish we hadn't started with the wrong people. They were godly and loved Jesus but had a different vision and capacity. We have learned to be patient and discerning and look for those who are: 1) Committed to following Jesus and 2) Committed to the vision He's given us.

19 I wish we had been more bold about speaking the truth into our core team's lives EARLIER and more persistently. We shouldn't have been afraid to confront those awkward moments because it was being done in love and for the health of the individuals and the church.

20 I wish I had celebrated the small victories along the way and kept a journal.

21 I wish I had enjoyed the time of quiet rest in between leaving out last ministry and beginning the busiest work of prelaunch.

THINGS I AM GLAD WE DID DO:

1   I am glad we have stuck to the vision the Lord gave us and the ministry he put in our hearts. It is easy to let people sway you into the way they think church should be and because you don't want to lose or offend them. I just pray we will always stand firm on the ministry God has given us.

2   I'm glad we learned to celebrate the small victories. Keep a Victory journal so you can see how far you have come and what God has done.

3   I'm glad we were not afraid to go to counseling for our marriage and for my husband to have a safe place to dump everything.

4   I'm glad we traveled with friends. Go on vacations with old friends from past ministries, college, childhood. Especially at first when no one knows you well enough to "get you." Hanging with people who love you and whom you love is super refreshing.

5   I'm glad we set boundaries on our hospitality. Have a clear boundary of what is and isn't OK. Of course you want your home to be welcoming, but especially if you have children, you may need to remember to make their needs in the home a priority.

6   I'm glad we have been consistent about taking a day off each week to rest from work, abide in God, and recreate ourselves for the rest of the week.

7 I'm glad we took a Sabbatical in year 7. My husband needed it, our family needed it, I needed it. It was a scary decision. Especially when you are not sure what you will come back to, but God was so faithful and all our people stepped up and grew in the process.

8 I'm glad my husband gave me plenty of time to truly be "all in" with the vision before any commitments were made.

9 I'm glad my husband reassured me that I and our children would always come before our ministry. That has provided an amazing foundation to allow for the craziness of life that is church planting.

10 I'm glad we turned our big, hard move into an "adventure" with our kids.

11 I'm glad we thought about what values we wanted to instill in our church plant's DNA: diversity, authenticity, unity and love. Then we knew what success looked like. Not based on numbers, but on our values.

12 I'm glad we went to a place we had a heart for.

13 I'm glad I tried for the best. Good, better, best, always pick the best!

14 I'm glad we scheduled vacations and breaks and excursions before planning big events for our church.

15 I'm glad my husband encourages our staff to play hard together because they work so hard together. All staff beach retreat with our families was amazing!

16 I'm glad we had our staff take a prayer day once a month. It instilled the right DNA in our baby church.

17 I'm glad we included the kids in both the ups and downs. They saw that real life has lows that are not insurmountable. They saw God's provisions and have more faith than us now!

18 I'm glad we trusted God with our finances and didn't try to save the church with our bank account.

19 I'm so glad we involved our kids in the decision making process, in everything we did.

20 I'm glad we started with community impact and truly knowing our community.

21 I'm glad we took Monday's off as a family in the beginning of launch.

22 I'm glad we dreamed big on community out reach events and had a goal so big that only God could accomplish it. He did it through people every time!

23 I'm glad I started a prayer journal and could see God more.

24 I'm glad I stepped out of my comfort zone and attended planter's wives retreats and established relationships with other women in the same position.

And there you have it. Some of our best do's and don'ts won in the school of hard knocks.

CONTRIBUTORS

Vanessa Bush, New City Christian Church, Albuquerque, NM - April 2010

Vanessa is wife to Nate and mom to Micah, Corban, and Evangline. In addition to supporting her husband and serving at church in various roles, Vanessa teaches high school English online. She loves drinking big cups of coffee, eating green chile, camping, hiking, and writing poetry on napkins.

Jennifer Fillinger, Hope Christian Church, New Orleans, LA - November 2008

Jennifer wouldn't want to live anywhere else. As a writer, jewelry maker, Jazzfest reveler and general Bohemian, the city (NOLA) suits her just fine and she is grateful God knew exactly who she was when He called her family there.

Jodi Harris, InRoads Church, Fremont, CA - 2001

Storyteller. Writer. Speaker. Teacher. Worship Leader. Church Planter. Pastor's Wife. Cool Mom. Jodi has had many roles since planting InRoads, but is currently the Women's Ministry Leader. She enjoys serving the women of InRoads and leading them to do "immeasurably more."

Holly Haulter, Catalyst Church, Greensboro, NC - October 2009

Holly and her husband Scott have 2 spunky little girls. As a family, they enjoy mixed martial arts, their dog, Scrappy, and all things Disney. Holly loves working with children, both in her psychology practice and as the Director of Children's Ministry at Catalyst.

MELISSA HOFMEISTER, LAKEPOINT CHURCH, MUSKEGO, WI – OCTOBER 2012

Melissa loves reading finance books, drinking high calorie coffee drinks, and hitting a fine art gallery with her husband. She is a mom of 3 boys, works part-time as the Associate Director of Recruitment for Stadia & serves as the First Impressions Leader at Lakepoint.

GAY IDLE, JOURNEY COMMUNITY CHURCH, FERNLEY, NV - SEPTEMBER 2009

Gay has worn many hats in her role as church planter; pastor's wife, mom, coffee table counselor, writer, vocal music coach, and women's ministry leader. Her passion is to have a heart captivated by the grace of Jesus.

DEBBIE JONES, JOHNSON CITY, TN, DIRECTOR OF SPOUSE AND FAMILY CARE FOR STADIA

Debbie and her husband, Tom, founded Princeton Community Church in Princeton, NJ (1992) and Southbrook Christian Church in Centerville, OH (1986). Debbie is the founder and leader of Bloom, a thriving ministry for Stadia spouses. Debbie loves spending time with family and friends and of course...chocolate ranks pretty high too!

JEN JONES, CITY CHURCH WINSTON, WINSTON-SALEM, NC - OCTOBER 2011

Jen is a wife, mother of 2, and works as the 'Task Ninja' as well as the Children's Director. She loves lattes, Jesus, singing, yoga, and giving hugs!

Jan Limiero, Life Journey Christian Church, Bakersfield, CA - October 2003

Jan loves church planting. It is the hardest thing She has ever done but also the adventure that has brought her closest to God. Two of Jan's favorite sports are rock climbing and caving. The highs and lows of church planting have surpassed both of those earthly thrills!

Janet McMahon, Restore Community Church, Kansas City, MO - March 2008

Janet is the mom of three children who are her daily joy. She serves as the Community Life Director at Restore equipping and empowering leaders of the church to disciple and develop one another while helping people find their way back to God.

Anne Milam, Kinetic Church, Charlotte, NC - February 2005

Anne is a leader, writer, wife, and mother of 4 wonderful children. She serves as the Children's Ministry Guru at Kinetic Church and leads disciples who make disciples. She enjoys reading, exercising, shopping and savoring dark chocolate. www.churchplantingwives.com

Vanessa Pugh, Velocity Church, Cleveland Ohio, planted April 2009

Vanessa loves helping pastors wives develop and grow in their role and she loves mentoring new believers. When she isn't leading the Connection Team at Velocity she loves hanging out with her family and coaching softball.

KRISTY ROBISON, ONE COMMUNITY CHURCH, DOUGLASVILLE, GA - MARCH 2011

Kristy enjoys spending time with her family, reading, and traveling. Kristy is an adoption/foster care advocate and believes that every child deserves a forever family. Kristy works as a Pre-k Director at a Christian School and volunteers at church and across the city.

SONDRA RUSH, CITYEDGE CHRISTIAN CHURCH, LAKEWOOD, OH, PLANTED - OCTOBER 2011

Sondra is married to Kevin Rush(who happens to be amazing), she's a blessed mother to three beautiful girls, and a Registered Nurse by trade. Sondra is passionate about discipling other women and helping them find their true identity in Christ.

KARA SIMPKINS, VARSITY CHURCH, CHAPEL HILL, NC - JANUARY 2011

Kara serves as Varsity's Children's Director and also leads the women's ministry. In addition, she works as an in-home personal trainer. She and Chad have 3 children and are looking forward to their family's continued adventures in church planting!

TAMMY SMITH, IMPACT COMMUNITY CHURCH, ELK GROVE CA - MARCH 2000

Tammy enjoys reading, taking naps and making memories with her family. She is the wife and support to her husband Barry Smith. Tammy is the children's director at Impact and loves kids.